THE SINGLE DAD'S GUIDE TO THE GALAXY

THE SINGLE DAD'S GUIDE TO THE GALAXY

Parenting in the Real World

ROGER McEWAN

Palmerston Press

Published by Palmerston Press

26 Marne Street
Palmerston North 4410
roger@mcewan.co.nz

First published 2017
Copyright © Roger McEwan, 2017

The right of Roger McEwan to be regarded as the author of this work in terms of the Copyright Act 1994 is hereby asserted.

All rights reserved. This book is copyright. Apart from fair dealing for the purpose of private study, research, criticism or review, permitted under the Copyright Act, no part may be reproduced by any process without the prior written permission of the publisher.

978-0-473-39232-1

Typeset and designed by Dana Brown, Smartwork Creative
Cover photography by Bernadette Peters, www.bernadettepeters.co.nz
Edited by Geoff Walker

To Rog and Liv
Too soon it will be time to fly

Contents

Introduction 9
1. Single 13
2. What Is a Single Dad? 22
3. Homeless 28
4. Our House 39
5. Muddling Through 46
6. Childcare 54
7. Fashion 62
8. The F Word, Alright? 70
9. Domesticity 78
10. The Bachelor Week 89
11. A Tale of Two Houses 99
12. School Holidays 114
13. A Woman's Touch 123
14. Fitness and Fatness 133
15. That's Entertainment 143
16. School 153
17. The Ex 165
18. Travelling 177
19. Money 185
20. Friends 195
21. Dating 203
22. Escaping 218
23. In the Thick of Things 226
24. Sons and Daughters 236
Epilogue 244

Introduction

One of the most valuable reflections that's come out of my experiences as a single dad is: *Have a great relationship with your ex.* I'd like to say have an outstanding one, a superb one, but I'm a realist and I imagine most people would settle for a great relationship. If you can do that, you'll make your life less complicated, troubled and stressful.

More importantly, it will enhance your children's lives because they're the ones stuck in the middle of your relationship with your ex, and they always will be. It's your children who suffer when you and your ex tangle in an effort to prove who's best or right.

So: Have a great relationship with your ex. This is obviously hard in the early days of a separation, especially if the split is acrimonious. But, over time, if you create an environment that allows wounds to heal then you can develop a great relationship. Yes it's hard, but it's not impossible.

This isn't a self-help book. I haven't been to the mountain where I discovered *the* answers that will let you, no matter what your personal circumstances, be the world's best single dad and have a fulfilling relationship with your children. Any book sold on that premise will ultimately prove to be a disappointment. There are many practical and constructive insights in this book which you can try, but I doubt you can learn how to be a great parent from just reading a book or taking a parenting course. They naturally help but I think you become a *better* parent by putting the lessons into practice and then learning from your own experience. When your children finally leave the nest you'll have either clocked up twenty years' parenting experience or one year's experience twenty times. It's entirely up to you.

Being able to reflect on and learn from your experiences is, I believe, one of the most important skills you can develop. People who have become great in any area of life didn't start out that way. No one is born great at anything. For most it's a slow, often painful, process over many long hours as they learn from their experiences and develop a sense of artistry.

So there's no book or course on *How to become a motor racing driver* or *Teach yourself to be a concert pianist*. That's not how the world works, even our accelerated, social-media-driven world in which the concept of delayed gratification seems merely an historical notion. Racing car drivers learn how to race by racing and how not to crash by crashing. Concert pianists learn through striking piano keys millions of times. There's no magic wand.

While I don't, and can't, have all the answers, what I do have is my story, my experiences and my insights, which I'm delighted to share. Unfortunately, or fortunately, they've all been learned the hard way through over seven years and counting as a single dad.

I hope my journey will give you a clearer appreciation for how single dads, and dads in general for that matter, see the world. Based on what you read I also hope you may decide to try to change your own world for the better. It could be how you interact with your ex, your current partner or your children. Maybe you'll simply try some of the ideas and see what happens. Advice and other people's experience becomes most valuable when you put it into practice.

Therefore this isn't a 'how to do it' book. It's a 'how I did it' book that I hope will help you think about 'how you're going to do it'. It's about how life worked, and at times didn't work, for my two beautiful, clever, funny, painful, messy, creative, exasperating, weird and lovely children – and, of course, me. Albert Einstein said insanity is doing the same things over and over and expecting different results. In that spirit I tried a lot of things. I kept what worked and abandoned the rest and managed to keep my sanity.

Everyone is different and every situation unique, so what has been successful for me may not be for you. What's important is that you reflect on what's happening in your own world and work out what's working and what isn't.

Like everyone who suddenly finds themselves in the position of being a single parent, I had no experience to fall back on. In the early days every aspect of my separation felt weird and alien and I often wondered how I'd cope. *If* I'd cope. I didn't have many single-dad friends whom I could turn to for advice, which strangely remains the case today.

I found out about life as a single dad as Liv, my daughter, used to say when she was little, 'all by self'. It's been through writing this book that I've come to the realisation that I've learnt far more about parenting and being a dad through being a single dad. I've experienced all the different roles you have to play when there's nobody else around: a parent, a dad, a father, a stand-in mum, a confidant, always a butler or maid, a teacher and, most crucially, a friend.

My hope is that you will find this book entertaining as well as enlightening. I've had many ups and downs, but on the whole it has been an epic adventure and nothing at all like an ordeal.

1. Single

Single: Unmarried or not involved in a stable sexual relationship.
www.Oxforddictionaries.com

At the time of completing this book, I've just turned fifty. I've had to keep changing that number as it's taken longer than I'd hoped to finish this book but, as you will see, I'm an optimist at heart. I've been a single dad for what feels like forever, but it's now just over seven years which made me forty-three when Rose, my ex-wife, and I separated.

Seven years as a single dad is seven years longer than I planned. When I said 'I do' with Rose, I did. I meant till death us do part, honouring, obeying and all the rest of the fine print. Rose and I spent sixteen years together and for the vast majority of the time we were a model, happy couple. We fought at times but which couples don't? Mostly it was as it was meant to be – loving and harmonious, and the children were always doted on.

One of the important facts about me is that I'm not famous. I'm not single-handedly raising my children in a mansion while coping with an unsympathetic media as I try to cure my addictions to sex, drugs and rock 'n' roll. Chance would be more than a fine thing. I'm trying to raise my children while working, studying, keeping the house clean, making lunches and dinners, writing and, right now, wondering how expensive it would be to be addicted to sex, drugs and rock 'n' roll.

I grew up and still live in Palmerston North, New Zealand, which can be charitably described as a great place to raise children and uncharitably as dull. It's not as bad as John Cleese, who was probably having a bad day, made out when he called it 'the suicide capital of New Zealand'. It's relatively small, with a population of around 80,000, but it's big enough to have all the amenities you need for a great family life – quality education, affordable housing and space in which to run and breathe. What it lacks is the dynamic pulse of a large city in which sports events, theatre, historic sites and the general hub-bub make you feel you're in the centre of the world.

Compensating for this, Palmerston North has few of the issues that plague large cities – pollution, over-crowding, lack of living space, unaffordable housing unless you're a millionaire, traffic, crime and, more recently and alarmingly, terrorism. Ordinary and typical are probably words that sum up Palmerston North.

Although I've lived here for most of my life, for a number of reasons I'm not a flag-waving fan. In fact it isn't really through choice that I'm here at all. I'm trapped and have been for years. First it was through career success when I briefly flirted with scrambling up the corporate ladder, and who wants to leave a promising career? Then came the arrival of children. It was a matter of considerable irony that just at the time my children came along, so did my redundancy notice nipping that promising corporate career in the bud. More about that later.

Rose and I have two children. Rog was born in 2000 and then Liv (Olivia) in 2001. Yes, Rog has the same name as me, and no, it wasn't part of a dynasty I'm trying to establish. *By heck there's been a Roger McEwan in the Manawatu for the last century, I'll have you know.* In fact, given some of the looks I've got over the years when Rog's name comes to light, I often wish we'd named him something different.

The story, and the absolute truth, is that after we had a mid-term ultrasound to make sure everything was okay, we discovered we were having a boy – 'Undoubtedly a boy' were the sonographer's actual flattering words. While Rose and I debated our first born's name, we started calling the emerging bump 'wee Rog'. After a few months of this, and in the absence of arriving at any other name that we could agree on, we named our new bundle of joy Roger. I've felt obliged to tell that story dozens of times.

As the children grew we decided to move out of the suburbs and bought a house on a huge section (1800sqm) on the outskirts of the city. That allowed us to kick back and relax or to charge around like lunatics, depending on the weather and everyone's mood. Our home had two large lounges, and the children's rooms were upstairs and incorporated a landing that was able to house all their toys. We renovated the kitchen – the 'we' part was me paying for someone to do the job right.

Our section also contained every sort of fruit tree you could imagine: peaches, apples, grapefruit, lemons, mandarins, tamarillos, figs, raspberries (which were divine), gooseberries, feijoas, blackberries, strawberries and red currants. Throw in a massive vegetable patch and we were in a prime location to raise children and pretty much follow in Tom and Barbara's footsteps and live *The Good Life*.

To earn a living, post my unexpected redundancy, I started my own consultancy business, McEwan and Associates Ltd, which I have been running now for over a decade. It sounds grander than it actually is as I'm the director, manager and consultant. In other words, it's just me and I don't really have a range of enthusiastic associates. What self-employment gives me is the ability to juggle work, family and study, and that's been invaluable for a single dad.

On the flip side, Palmerston North isn't exactly the corporate capital of anywhere, and so I've had to turn my hand to a variety of tasks as well as hit the road from time to time in order to keep cash, the life blood of any business, rolling in. My main business interest, and love, is strategic management, which I also study and teach, although strategy contracts are rare. Not many people understand what strategic management is, fewer still in Palmerston North it seems.

On the surface everything was idyllic but, to cut a long story short, the relationship storms came and in mid-2008 Rose and I separated. Marriage that ends without someone dying, of natural causes that is, is often branded a failure but I think that's wrong. My marriage didn't fail, it simply didn't last. Rose and I aren't failures, we are successful, older and wiser parents and adults. Therefore my children aren't from a broken home, they're from two loving homes. Having both parents under the same roof is, I think, a pretty weak measure of relationship success or of a positive home environment.

Like everyone, Rose and I entered into our marriage and raising a family with no thought of what life might be like if it didn't work out. Anyone having those thoughts shouldn't wander down the aisle in the first place. In New Zealand when you separate you remain married in the eyes of the law. The only grounds for divorce is two years' separation. Therefore it was my newly acquired 'lack of a stable sexual relationship' that found me classified, for the first time in a decade and a half, as single. Only this time a single dad.

I'm curious: what images come to mind when you picture a single dad looking after his children? Many people would imagine the scene as a bit of a shemozzle – the stereotype of a hassled grumpy dad yelling as the frozen dinner burns in the kitchen. I have had days like that, but they are memorable because they are the exception and nothing remotely like the rule.

Being a dad isn't a chore either, something to be endured until I can mercifully drop my children back to their mum where they will be cared for properly and I can get on with my real life. It makes me wonder how much sharing, or more accurately off-loading, parental responsibilities is a driver for seeking a new partner. That will likely end in tears for all concerned.

BEHIND THE SCENES

To give you an idea of how things play out in our home, here is a typical scene. Family time in the McEwan home, take 1 …

INTERIOR (INT). MCEWAN HOME, LOUNGE – NIGHT
The lounge is warm and well lit. LIV is sitting on the couch, hypnotised by the TV with her feet tucked underneath her. A chef burbles away off screen and there is the faint sound of gunfire. The far door opens. DAD enters and walks between LIV and the TV.

> **DAD**
> (Loudly)
> Bedtime and teeth.

DAD exits through the near door. LIV, taking no notice, remains hypnotised by the TV.

INT. MCEWAN HOME, OFFICE – NIGHT
ROG sits behind a computer fully engaged with whatever is on the screen. The sound of gunfire is loud. The chef can be heard faintly in the background. DAD enters and stares at ROG.

> **ROG**
> (Staring at his computer)
> No.

ROG keeps playing, DAD remains still. DAD looks thoughtful then, smiling, slowly turns and exits.

INT. MCEWAN HOME, LOUNGE – NIGHT
DAD re-enters the lounge and moves closer to LIV who still hasn't moved.

> **DAD**
> (Sweetly)
> Bedtime, little one.
>
> **LIV**
> (Jumping up)
> Hug.

LIV lunges at DAD who catches her, spins her around and starts marching her out the door.

> **DAD**
> Teeth.

INT. MCEWAN HOME, HALLWAY – NIGHT

DAD is marching LIV towards the bathroom.

> **LIV**
> (Spinning around, demanding but friendly)
> Huggggg!

DAD, looking resigned, pauses then hugs LIV who, smiling, exits into the bathroom. The shot tracks into the bathroom where LIV is cleaning her teeth.

> **ROG**
> (Off screen, whispered)
> The Father.

DAD turns and ROG gently connects with a jab to the stomach.

> **DAD**
> Mind the abs, mate.

> **ROG**
> You mean the flabs.

> **DAD**
> (Getting into a karate sparring pose)
> Hilarious. Look as good when you are my age, I think not.

> **ROG**
> (Hands up, backs into his room and closes the door)
> No, no.

DAD waits. ROG'S door is closed. LIV is cleaning her teeth.

> **DAD**
> (Loudly)
> Half hour reading time.

DAD exits. ROG emerges in pyjamas and enters the bathroom, where LIV is still cleaning her teeth.

INT. MCEWAN HOME, LOUNGE – NIGHT

DAD turns off TV, mercifully shutting up the chef, who is describing how to make a jus. DAD breathes out in relief and sits down where LIV was sitting. Silence.

> **LIV**
> (Off camera)
> Move, butthead.
>
> **ROG**
> (Off camera)
> You're the butthead, Hobbit.
>
> **LIV**
> (Off camera, louder)
> Daaaaad. *It* won't get out of the way.
>
> **ROG**
> Shut it, Fatty.

DAD gently shaking his head and smiling. Two doors can be heard closing.

> **DAD**
> (Very loudly)
> Reading, not games. I'll be in to check.

DAD lies down flat on the couch and closes his eyes.

INT. MCEWAN HOME, LIV'S BEDROOM THIRTY MINUTES LATER – NIGHT

LIV is in bed reading a Jacqueline Wilson book. DAD sweeps into the room but stops frowning, looking at the mess.

> **DAD**
> (Shaking head)
> Disgraceful.
>
> **LIV**
> (Yawning)
> Hey, it's creative.

DAD kicks clothes out of the way and tucks LIV into bed. LIV'S arms emerge and she hugs DAD and won't let go. DAD tickles LIV and she lets go.

> **DAD**
> Good night.
>
> **LIV**
> Good night, Dad.

DAD turns out the light and exits. Shot tracks with DAD.

> **LIV**
> (Calling out off camera)

> I love you.

DAD
(Calling out behind him)
I love you too.

INT. MCEWAN HOME, ROG'S BEDROOM – NIGHT

ROG is in bed reading a Sherlock Holmes book. DAD enters the room, stops and surveys the room and grunts.

ROG
(Continues reading)
What?

DAD harpoons his book with a modified karate strike and then fakes a strike to ROG'S stomach.

ROG
(Shaking his head)
Bad father.

DAD smiling, puts a bookmark in the book and adds it to a pile next to the bed. DAD surveys ROG'S bed, shaking his head.

ROG
What?

DAD
(Still shaking his head)
It's a dog's dinner.

ROG
No it isn't, it's very comfy.

DAD
Hmmm. Good night.

ROG
Good night.

DAD turns out the light and exits.

INT. MCEWAN HOME, HALLWAY – NIGHT

Dad turns on the CD PLAYER and classical music (Mendelssohn) starts softly playing. DAD exits.

SCENE FADES – END

Normal: that's the word that encapsulates that scene. It's hard to remember exactly how it worked before I became a single dad. I'm sure it was roughly the same except blended with Rose's voice as well and, as Rog and Liv were much smaller, there was probably a little less attitude floating around. Having two parents on duty was a luxury I didn't fully appreciate at the time. They were the good old days alright. The children were in bed, and asleep, by 7.30pm. Heaven.

The nicest compliment I receive from time to time is not related to my work, study or writing – it is when someone calls me a great dad. I've worked hard to hear those words and I'm certain that I'm a much better dad, parent, father and person than the one who abruptly found himself lacking a stable sexual relationship back at the beginning.

2. What Is a Single Dad?

Every father should remember that one day his son will follow his example instead of his advice.
Charles Kettering (inventor, engineer, businessman, 1876–1958)

I'd like to think I'm a typical single dad but, to be honest, I don't know if that's right. From what I have seen, read and heard, we don't know much about single dads. The majority of books are closer to manuals on the subject such as *The Single Father: A dad's guide to parenting without a partner*. These books tell us nothing about single dads but instead focus on what they consider to be the right way to be a single dad.

As I've said, I have grave doubts that you can learn to be a great dad that way in exactly the same way reading *Fifty Shades of Grey* won't make you a more proficient, dynamic and exciting lover. It will definitely give you some ideas to try, unless you are already very close to the edge, but you do have to give them a go. To become a better parent you have to spend time being a parent.

Josh Wolf was closer to looking at the life of a single dad with his entertaining autobiographical book *It Takes Balls – Dating single moms and other confessions from an unprepared single dad*. But while initially it seems to reflect on the life of a single dad, ultimately, it seems to me, the focus is on dating and all that entails. It was hard to find much parenting between Josh's wild escapades.

There are also books in the romantic genre where the lady next door covets the tall, dark and handsome single dad and is waiting for the chance for him to come over to check out her muffins. Judging by that last sentence I think I could write something like that but it would require imagination and not reflection as life isn't like that. At least my life isn't.

Coming back to reality, if I had to summarise what the world thinks about single dads, it seems closer to the stereotypical portrayal of someone waltzing in and out of their children's lives, fitting them in around work while trying to attract attention at the local bar, usually unsuccessfully. If that feels about right, then I'm here to demonstrate that it's wrong! If that's typical, then thankfully I'm not typical. There are bound to be dads like that, just as there are stereotypical sleazy, boozy businessmen, and I'm not one of those either. But the problem with stereotypes is that they are powerful and require little evidence to keep them entrenched.

When I was researching the world's view of single dads I stumbled across a blog written by a divorced single mom (she was American). She had posted six points about single dads, which she described as though they're common knowledge, almost self-evident:

- Single dads are often inexperienced at multi-tasking.
- Single dads don't get to live with their kids.
- Single dads often feel left out of things.
- Single dads can become insecure about parenting.
- Single dads are working and trying to parent at the same time.
- Single dads can't be mom.

I felt obliged to comment and posted the following response, which I've edited slightly so it makes sense.

- Human beings can't multi-task, we can only task-switch. It is thought that females are better at this but I remain sceptical. What's more, you get better at everything with practice.
- Many single dads like myself share care fifty-fifty and live with their children just as much as single mums.
- You don't have to be left out of things regarding your children if you choose not to. Rose and I communicate well and make sure we both know what is happening and when, because we know it's our children who suffer the consequences of mix-ups.
- Parents in general can be insecure about parenting, even when there are two of them. It is nice to have another adult to be insecure with but that doesn't make it gender-specific.
- Many single mums also work and parent as I did before we separated. So, no change there.
- And being mom? Maybe. Probably. Okay, yes. My feminine side is still pretty masculine! But single mums can't be dad either, no matter how many power tools they buy.

Reading between the lines, it appears that the thinking I was responding to is stuck in the 1950s when mums did the vast majority of the parenting. But the world has changed and thankfully it's even evolved a little. The majority of the dads I know are involved with all aspects of their children's lives and so they're able to cope if they find themselves solo either temporarily or permanently. I was hands-on with my children from the very start, and so looking after my children without help wasn't a culture shock. I'm even okay at looking after myself – I don't require mothering.

So what I want to achieve with this book is to bring reality to the discussion, at least a little bit of *my* reality. I want you to see through my eyes and glimpse inside my head, that of a responsible single dad. You will see how the children and I adapted to this new environment and transitioned quickly from surviving to thriving. I hope you get a different perspective – a real perspective – and start to rethink what the term single dad suggests.

That's what I *want* to achieve, but what I'd *love* to achieve is to make all parents who are struggling with children, their exes or current partners to stop and reflect – hopefully in that order. This book may be written from the perspective of a single dad but I think many of the insights can be applied equally to any situation where two people are sharing the care of children, together or separated.

The easiest action you can take right now to improve the world of you and your children is not to start doing anything new – it's more likely you should stop doing some of the old. I'm referring to those behaviours that you have been polishing for years that create frustration, conflict, stress, anxiety and doubt.

I have met many parents in my travels and some of their stories are as baffling as they are tragic. In particular, two men stand out in my mind whose behaviour is self-centred and destructive yet they're oblivious to the bleak future they're creating. They put themselves first and either happily or ignorantly use their children as a tool to manipulate and bully their exes to get their own way. It seems they believe they have an entitlement to the lives of their partners, who should do everything they dictate. If they continue to behave in this way, it's likely that when their children are old enough they'll want little to do with them. Sadly, they'll be alone and left wondering why.

So please, stop and reflect and ask that simplest of all questions – what am I trying to achieve? Edwards Deming insightfully wrote that it is not necessary to change, survival is not mandatory. Nor is having fun or giving your children the best start in life – but it's by far the most preferable.

Now you know what I'm trying to achieve. What I'm trying to avoid is harming anyone during the telling of my story. Unfortunately I can't say that no one was harmed during the making of it. Separation and divorce inflict both direct damage and collateral damage, but this story is more about fun, healing and making the world a slightly better place. It's my story and I want all those involved, including my children and Rose, to be able to enjoy reading it and not cringe, feel incensed or think WTF. That has been challenging at times!

ABOUT ME

Before I get fully into stride, I must tell you more about my personal circumstances. Otherwise parts of the story won't make sense. In particular I need to explain why I stayed a single dad without bothering to date for a number of years. The salient points are somewhat convoluted, but I will try to communicate them succinctly and clearly.

Not long after my separation I started a relationship with Cathy (not her real name) who, I hasten to add, had nothing to do with the separation. The complicating factor was that she lived in England. But this isn't one of those cautionary tales about internet relationships in which people travel across continents in search of love only to get ripped off or end up in prison after the stash of drugs in the 'I Love You' chocolate is discovered.

Cathy and I had spent time together in our twenties, long before Rose and I were Rose and I. I knew Cathy very well. We got back in touch during the separation and it was like winding the clock back, things just seemed to fall into place despite the distance. So although we were separated by 11,000 miles with children on both sides of the planet, we became a sort-of-couple and started considering how that might work in the future. More of the details will emerge from time to time as required, but in a nutshell that's why I didn't dive back into the singles scene with obscene haste.

Another aspect you need to understand is the care arrangement Rose and I created for our children. From day one, Rose and I agreed to share the care of the children fifty-fifty. This was a no-brainer for both of us as we had both been hands-on parents and neither wanted to take a back seat in our children's lives. We also knew that they still needed as much of Mum and Dad as they could get, maybe even more now as they were still rather young – Rog was eight and Liv was six.

A quick point of clarification is also needed here. I'm a single dad but the fifty-fifty care arrangement means my children are still being raised by both parents. It is now like a tag team arrangement. This means that it's more balanced than many – maybe the majority – of so-called nuclear families.

The one aspect of my story I don't intend to cover in any detail is Rose and my separation. I see no purpose in dragging you, me or anyone else back through that unhappy time. Like most separations the story is sad and hard. I did write a couple of chapters about it and, although it was cathartic to write, the words are best left for another time as they only get in the way. Take my word for it, it wasn't fun for anyone.

So welcome as the story begins in earnest.

It's June 2008 and it's the middle of winter in Palmerston North. Chris Brown's 'Forever' is ironically at number one and I have just become a single dad. Although the story starts in 2008, I didn't start putting pen to paper until late 2012 – the spur for this will become apparent as the story unfolds. But I kept a blog in which I captured my thinking as life unfolded. It made interesting reading in retrospect, and I'd managed to capture a lot of the stories and reflections that I've used in this book.

3. Homeless

All changes are more or less tinged with melancholy, for what we are leaving behind is part of ourselves.
Amelia Barr (British novelist, 1831-1919)

Anyone who's separated will know about the chaos it brings. Almost overnight you go from settled and ordered – although probably not all that content – to confused and chaotic. After sixteen years together, Rose and my lives seemed intractably linked. Trying to split things down the middle proved to be a nightmare.

We started by working our way through the financial aspects and negotiating who would have what. We agreed early on that she would keep the house and buy me out. On reflection it wasn't quite a negotiated decision but more a matter of that's the way the chips fell. I'd moved out, and Rose was living in the house and wanted to stay. So it seemed the right thing to do.

For the first time in my entire life I didn't have a home address. That was the first thing I needed to rectify, and fast. I was forty-three, but having just left home I felt closer to twenty. I'd taken some of my clothes, but in those first few days that was all I had to my name. It was a surreal feeling.

Initially I stayed at my mum's house, which made me feel closer to sixteen. That felt preferable to the houses of friends whom I hoped wouldn't have yet heard about the separation. But after living back at home for only six days I was starting to go a little crazy. It wasn't my mum's fault, it was situational. I wanted a quiet space to think things through but she and my older brother, who was also living there at that stage, seemed starved of conversational variety.

Rental property is thankfully abundant in Palmerston North as it's a university city. I found a house near to the children's school on John F. Kennedy Drive and moved in as quickly as possible. It was a modern townhouse with a tiny yard and garden, and this suited me. Although I love gardening, I had no desire to invest time maintaining someone else's garden. To compensate for the lack of outdoor space, the house was opposite an impressively large park which was complete with a small playground about twenty metres from our front door. This was perfect for letting the children, and me, burn off energy. We often played ball tag with Muffin, a yellow smiley-face ball Liv had picked up on her travels.

It was only going to be a short-term home and, as such, it worked well. I was planning on buying a house as soon as financially practical. In this respect I was fortunate that the Palmerston North property market wasn't experiencing one of the bubbles that have made buying a house unaffordable in many cities. If you find yourself unable to re-enter the property market after separation, which must be common, I suggest you aim to rent in the best location you can.

The children were also changing schools, a decision Rose and I had made previously that was now somewhat up in the air. We made the decision based on the situation at the time, but in hindsight it would probably have been wiser to have left them at their current school, given the separation. The original reasons for switching schools hadn't gone away and I think we just carried on while we sorted things out. With the change of school, any house I bought would ideally be close to their new school.

Like many countries, New Zealand employs a school zoning system. To get your children into the school you want, you have to live in, or at least own (which I think is cheating), a house in the school's catchment zone. This makes house buying often a strategic decision for parents. The school system in New Zealand is, on the whole, reasonably good, but anyone who thinks there is no difference between a decile ten school (in a more affluent area) and a decile one school (in a less affluent area) is wrong.

As Rose was keeping the house, she was also keen on keeping everything in it as well. This made sense, but it left me with few possessions. I ended up taking a TV (our older one and not the flash, cinematic, all-the-bells-and-whistles one I'd recently, and lovingly, installed), my dust-gathering gym equipment, clothes, books and a few pieces of unrequired furniture.

On the plus side, it was the quickest and easiest house move I'd ever been involved with. But after I had unpacked everything, my lack of worldly goods was starkly highlighted. No matter which way I looked, all I could see was carpet – and there was nowhere to sit or sleep.

Although our former joint possessions were part of the financial agreement – and here's a lesson I hope you never have to learn – there is a quantum difference between current and replacement value. The process Rose and I followed was to wander through the house and agree on a *current* value for all our possessions. Most of these had been built up over the previous sixteen years and while some were on the old side, they were all in good working condition. The result of this was that we gave most items a fairly conservative value. For example, the $2000 Sony stereo which was eight years old but was still able to crank out the music was given a value in the vicinity of $300.

The current value of all our possessions we estimated at around $15,000, which we then split fifty-fifty. The fact that we had our contents insured for closer to $60,000 should have a sounded a warning bell for me, but I missed this in the general confusion of the time.

The lesson I learnt, blindingly obvious in hindsight, was that you can't replace half your possessions with half their *current* value. In fact half their current value allows you to replace only a fraction of what you had. Valuing everything using a replacement value would have been as wrong, although in my favour, and so I recommend a middle-ground approach. As hard as it may be, split your actual possessions equally so each person ends up with half the old and has to replace the other half with new. In that way there is no need to value anything. The situation I found myself in wasn't anyone's fault and it made sense at the time. Throw in the unavoidable feelings of guilt for my part in the whole episode and I was happy to bend as far as possible in the misguided belief that this would somehow make things right – or at least righter. Of course it didn't.

I was left with $7500 to turn my rented house into a home in which the children and I could feel relaxed and comfortable. I needed beds (x3), bedroom furniture (x3), furniture for the lounge and dining room, appliances, pictures, glasses, cutlery, linen, art, whiteware, tools, knick-knacks, food, etc.

As it dawned on me that I had painted myself neatly into a corner, I also realised that I had little choice of action as the children were due in three days. I was going to have to buy everything at some stage, and as I'd worked hard on maintaining a decent credit history I rushed out armed with plastic. I hired a refrigerator, washing machine, dryer and lounge suite based on the logic that I had no idea what any future house might need in terms of size and style. I then went on a credit card shopping spree to turn the rental house into a home. I appreciate that this option isn't available to everyone and so you may need to think creatively and beg, borrow but please don't steal.

STARTING OVER

As I ploughed through all the tasks needed to establish our new home, Cathy and I kept in regular contact. She had been through a similar divorce experience and had some of her own hard-earned lessons to share. While I had a fifty-fifty shared-care arrangement, she had something closer to a ninety-five to five split. Although most lessons are available only in hindsight, before you consider having a family, or even agreeing to devote yourself to someone for the rest of your life, ask yourself this question: if our relationship turns to custard what involvement would this person want to have in their children's future? If you think the answer is less than 30 per cent I would give them elbow, *tout de suite.*

The twelve-hour time difference between England and New Zealand meant we spoke either first thing in the morning or late in the evening. Although I was physically alone, it meant that I did have someone in my corner with whom I could chat, get advice and bounce issues and ideas. This made the post-separation trials and tribulations a little bit easier. There aren't many pluses to a long-distance relationship, but in the early days it gave me emotional support without having to complicate the children's lives further with a potential replacement mother figure.

After a few weeks in the new house, the children and I started to settle into the new routine, at least on the surface. If I take myself back to those days, I remember that they were tense and strained, and goodness knows what the children were thinking. On reflection, we were all coping while we waited for the new normal to arrive. I'd like to think now that this came quickly but I know it's easy to reinterpret the past based on the outcome of an event rather than on the event itself. We're fine now so we must have been fine then too.

Rose and I decided that it would be easiest for everyone if the children swapped houses on Sundays at 6pm. That, incidentally, sounds like a pleasant exchange over a cup of tea rather than the awkward email exchange it was in reality. But the decision made perfect sense and meant that the children would not have their school week or weekend disrupted. The parent 'on duty' would be aware of all the school and after-school events that needed to be organised and could pass the information over with the children and all their belongings.

The logistics of this new arrangement worked well and the children and their associated paraphernalia were swapped at 6pm, usually on the dot. When Rog and Liv were dropped off at my house we quickly put away clothes and toys and then, if it was nice evening, we would pop over to the park and play or, if it was wet, play a game or watch a DVD. What didn't work so well – and probably to be expected – was the communication. I would often find out that the coming week contained an event, such as a fancy-dress day, with minimal notice. 'I want to be a fairy princess,' Liv would inform me and Rog would apparently '*need* to be a robot'. No pressure.

As a parent you just want your child to blend in at school, and so you move mountains to achieve the fairy princess and robot look, cursing under your breath the entire time. Rose and I get on famously now but it wasn't always so convivial, and situations like this tested our restraint. It went both ways. I was left in no doubt when my actions had annoyed Rose. Accidentally of course.

Two houses meant two home environments, and Rose and I carried on parenting as we saw fit. In the main, as we had been together for sixteen years we weren't poles apart and the children got much the same treatment at both houses. They basically got a dad flavour and a mum flavour.

VERTIGO

When the children were with me, I had everything under control the majority of the time, but there was the odd anxiety-inducing obstacle that appeared mountainous. For example, I remember worrying that getting the children to different sports in the weekend was going to be a logistical impossibility, but usually it was resolved simply.

Personally I don't like calling on favours from friends, maybe it's a male trait, but every now and again I needed to. Gradually things became easier, and being able to debrief with Cathy and get her perspective was invaluable. The children appeared to be settling well into this new world and seemed to be showing no signs of adjustment issues. And that goes to prove we often see what we want to see.

I was playing a game with Liv. This was not long after the separation, so she was six. I can't remember what game we were playing, as we had loads of board games, but she wanted to play again. I explained to her that I needed to get dinner ready and so I went into the kitchen and she wandered off to her room.

It was unlike her not to follow me into the kitchen – she has always been my shadow – and so a few minutes later I poked my nose into her room to see what she was doing. She wasn't in her room. I checked the toilet and then the other rooms (there weren't that many), but there was no sign of her.

Ice snaked through my veins.

With no sign of her in the house I double-timed outside and performed a hasty lap of the house. Nothing. I visually searched the playground but it was empty, meaning that at least she hadn't crossed what was a busy street by herself. Back in the house I was struggling to make sense of the situation. It was as if I'd closed my eyes and seconds later when I'd reopened them the world had changed colour.

With blood pounding in my ears, I rechecked her room and that was when I heard soft sobs coming from the wardrobe. I opened the door and there she was, sitting in the dark crying.

I felt a wave of relief and then a more powerful wave of guilt. Now it could have been that Liv was simply being a brat when she didn't get her way. Maybe. In fact on reflection that's pretty plausible, but on that 2008 spring evening I certainly didn't see it that way. It felt like evidence of damage – inflicted by me.

The children had been coping on the surface, but clearly all was not well. I recalled that Liv had said a few days earlier in a sad tone 'Mum and Dad don't live together any more', but I had just hugged her, thinking it was a momentary thought. I had been focusing on the activities of our new life and not on life itself. I realised that a lot of effort would be needed if the children were going to blossom in this new foreign environment.

I cuddled her, and when she stopped crying I piggy-backed her out to the lounge and popped her on the couch. I wrapped her in a blanket with her favourite teddy bears and put on a DVD while I returned to the kitchen to finish making dinner.

That's when the world really lurched and the kitchen walls started closing in on me. On reflection, I'm certain I was experiencing the closest thing I have ever had – and ever hope to have – to a panic attack. A feral feeling of desperation came over me. This time I had to fight hard against a strong desire for flight. I took long, slow, deep breaths but still felt breathless, so I rustled the children off to the playground, displaying what I hoped would be seen as excitement. This helped lighten Liv's mood which, in turn, made me start to feel better.

At the playground I got the air, space and time I needed. The world stopped reeling so violently, but I was left with the pounding thought that I couldn't do this. It was ridiculous. I couldn't be a single dad.

As I sat there watching Rog and Liv yahooing around the playground, I completely and irrationally doubted my ability to cope. It was a powerful feeling that had a stark clarity to it. Rose would have to look after the children and I would become a weekend dad as was more traditional. If that also meant becoming a fat alcoholic womaniser, so be it.

I can't recollect much about that night's dinner, but I must have fed the children, supervised teeth brushing and tucked them into bed as normal. Later I was able to talk to Cathy and found myself dumping the story on her. She was, as always, wonderfully calm, and it rubbed off. I felt I was heading back to something like my usual optimistic, happy, confident self, albeit slightly dented. I found the simple process of saying things out loud hugely beneficial.

REGGIE

As I drove the children to school the next day that old saying 'Whatever doesn't kill you makes you stronger' popped into my head. I sure wasn't dead, and I'd achieved insight into where my effort needed to go. Not into the logistics, but into the children and into myself.

Then I did what I often do in these situations – I sought out information about what was really happening. I went to the public library and found a couple of useful-looking books as well as locating some informative websites. New Zealand websites such as Man Alive are excellent and informative but be careful when searching as when you type in 'single dad', Google assumes you're looking to date.

What I found from the books and online – and this is what I often find – is that what I was going through was entirely normal. My experiences and feelings were typical and there were, apparently, loads of people throughout the world at different places on the same road. Phew! That alone was enormously reassuring. There's a real comfort in knowing you are not alone.

By way of analogy, I once noticed that my calf muscles were twitching and that they appeared to be housing something snake-like. I was moderately concerned, but I freaked Liv out when I showed her while we were watching *Doctor Who*. I Googled 'twitching calf muscles' and, sure enough, there are a bunch of us with that as well. Laying off alcohol seemed to be the common recommendation. I hate that advice.

I returned home with my books and spent the morning reading about separation and its effects on children and what I could/should be doing. As it was nearing lunchtime I decided to work from home for the rest of the day, which is usually a euphemism I use for bunking off. But that gave me the opportunity to meet Regina, who literally floated into my life and became part of my journey.

I was in the lounge, cross-legged on the floor (which doubled as my desk at the time), checking emails. I was unshaven and dressed in shorts and a T-shirt, looking every inch unemployed and nothing like a business consultant. For background noise I had a TV music channel playing. I love working to music. Classical for when I have to think hard or I'm trying to be creative (like now), and rock and pop for tasks I can do in my sleep. A song came on that captured my attention for two reasons: it was catchy and I recognised the tune from a TV ad. It was, I discovered, Regina Spektor (Reggie) singing 'Fidelity', which contained the very catchy piece that had been used in the ad. It's impossible for me to communicate how it sounds without singing it and you have been spared this fate by the fact that this is a book. However, I'm keen to make this into an audio book, in which case I will have the opportunity to sing. I hope I do it justice, but history suggests I won't. In the interim you can find the song easily on the internet if you feel inclined.

When you find music you love there's a tendency to think everyone will love it as well. I tried to share this love and pushed Reggie too hard and too often on my children. They liked her initially, but now they cry out in pain if I put her music on in the car (which they still do today. Sorry, Reggie).

With Reggie singing in the background, the children and I meandered onwards and, as it turned out, upwards. I have heard that children can still hold on to the hope that their parents will get back together long after it's obvious they won't, sometimes well into adulthood. My children never asked me that tough question; maybe it was obvious that we wouldn't. But becoming aware of information like this helped me develop a much larger and fuller picture of my situation. Being aware of what was happening gave me a fighting chance of seeing the issues and acting earlier to avoid larger issues and crises.

The major lesson for me was that I couldn't any more be a dad who was focused only on a part of the children's world. When the children were with me I needed to be both a dad and a sort of mum, providing the full range of parenting and not just getting the logistics right. I had been, I considered, a great dad – but now what was required was learning to be a great dad and a great parent.

Reflections

- When you are dividing up your possessions, think through how you can value them so each partner is treated fairly. It isn't a game you are trying to win – adults act fairly.
- Set up your new house so your children feel at home. You're going to spend the money anyway and so, if you can, try to get as much done up front as possible.
- Try to maintain the same, or similar, routines for your children in both homes. In this way they won't equate change-overs with upheaval.
- Don't forget your children's emotional needs as you battle through all the logistical changes.
- If you are going to operate a fifty-fifty arrangement, a 6pm handover on Sundays may work well for everyone.
- Getting information about what you are going through will help you regain control. The library, internet and single parents are great sources of information and support.
- Having a confidant who has your best interests at heart is priceless.
- Finding the right soundtrack for this part of your life can help through the turbulent times. Give Regina Spektor a try.

4. Our House

Anyone who lives within their means suffers from a lack of imagination.
Oscar Wilde (playwright, novelist and poet, 1854–1900)

The hire company that I used to equip the house with whiteware had a special deal: for one dollar a month I hired a white, trendy-in-the-60s vinyl couch. I was delighted with the deal but Cathy, when I emailed through a photo, pronounced it perfectly hideous. Still, looks aside it was the only place in the house, apart from the bedroom, where you could lie down. For that reason I loved it, even though my feet dangled over the edge.

One evening when I was without the children, feeling absolutely knackered after karate and reflective about the world in general, I was sprawled on my one-dollar-a-month couch. Karate is a hobby that you can become addicted to. The sweat, the intensity, the focus and discipline either send you packing after one or two sessions or entice you to return week after week. At the time I was a devotee.

I discovered karate after the children started training at a local club when they were seven and eight. I loved watching them during the hour-long lesson because it was pure entertainment, like a scene from a martial arts comedy: cute little boys and girls bouncing around like miniature Bruce Lees. To generate spirit and intensity when they kick or punch the children are encouraged to *kiai* (pronounced *key I*), which translates roughly 'to shout'. In their shy, high-pitched voices they usually whisper *kiai,* meaning they actually whisper the word 'shout'. They were very cute but not very scary.

My children enjoyed karate at first but it was intense and they lost interest after six months – Rog in general and Liv after she received a kick to her solar plexus during a tournament which had her in tears. I swept my six-year-old up in my arms and she was quickly restored to health through the miraculous healing properties of ice cream.

The karate instructor, a former New Zealand champ, was an old school friend. He was happy for me to attend the adult session and, in his words, 'give it a thrash'. I did and I loved it. I found that when you're practising karate your problems and worries and your current world fade from focus. You become fully engaged coping with the physical requirements of maintaining technique and not getting smacked in the ear. The only people in your world are you, the instructor and anyone standing directly in front of you. If your mind wanders you can be snapped back to the present by blocking a blow with your head – which isn't recommended.

Back to me on the couch, knackered and reflective.

It's stating the obvious but an advantage of being with someone, as opposed to being in a long-distance relationship, is that you can see them. I'm confident if Cathy had seen me that night she would have left me in peace. The phone, our way of keeping in touch, doesn't allow that luxury and I must have sounded exactly like I felt, tired and unenthusiastic. The topic we were discussing was my lack of progress towards buying a house. Given my attitude, Cathy determined the corrective action required was a decent kick up the backside. So to accompany the actual kicking from karate, I got an equally solid virtual kicking. In hindsight I probably did need a rev up, just not *that* night.

The separation and financial settlement meant that I had money in the bank. But, as many lottery winners can attest, it can evaporate quickly. I mumbled a few assurances about getting onto it, the best I could do at the time, but my lack of enthusiasm obviously shone through. Cathy's tone and sentences became clipped and teacher-esque. I was left in no doubt that we would be revisiting the subject sooner than later. But in my case a good night's sleep is often all that separates apathy from action and the next day I felt ready to spring into action.

HOUSE HUNTING

Rose and I didn't alter our decision to switch the children's school despite the separation intervening. Therefore if one of us wasn't living in the new school zone, and Rose was miles from the boundary, we would be added to the notoriously large group labelled 'outside of zone'. Then we would need luck to be allocated a place. Relying on the school being under-subscribed was a big risk. I thought the fact that my brother and I were both 'old boys' would be taken into account, but it was pointed out to me – by both Rose and Cathy – that the application form had no place in which to record this information. It was a clear oversight on the school's part, in my opinion, but that didn't help our situation. Therefore house hunting began in earnest.

Generally I behave like a typical male, and I'm somewhat proud of it. For example, I don't try on dozens of items in different shops when clothes shopping. I know what I like and once I see it it's then merely a matter of fit. It's a similar story with cars. In my life I've taken around five cars for test drives and have bought around five cars. I do my homework, sometimes well, and then I buy. The test drive is simply to confirm that the wheels stay on and the car doesn't drive like a lemon.

Buying a house is different and I was aware I needed to be thorough. Even though I was hunting by myself, because houses are listed online, it meant that when I found one of interest I was able to send the link to Cathy so we could discuss its features. After employing this process for a few weeks I had been through about ten houses, both online and in person, and they were okay, but only okay. None of them had a wow factor, or if they did they had an equivalent ouch factor in terms of price or location. Just as my enthusiasm was waning, an attractive house, ideally situated, came onto market. It was literally around the corner from the children's new school and zoned for the future schools Rose and I had discussed. It seemed perfect.

I missed the open home the following Sunday as I was playing golf, maybe getting my priorities wrong, and so I did a dangerous thing. I contacted the realtors directly and expressed my interest – which is the equivalent of kicking a hungry crocodile to get his/her attention. A time to view the house was hurriedly organised and the next day I was met at the gate by a blonde, well-dressed, attractive, presumably single (I just happened to notice) real-estate agent. As we introduced ourselves I felt a sense of disappointment from Ms/Miss Realtor. I often facilitate groups in work situations and I've become experienced at reading people's body language. Ms Realtor looked nonplussed which I found strange as I was dressed in a suit doing what I considered to be a decent impression of a well-healed, motivated buyer.

'Is anyone else coming?' She asked politely but coolly.

'No, there isn't,' I said, trying to mask my wariness with enthusiasm.

'Oh right. Let's get started then.'

We went on the usual tour-de-house, which is inevitably an awkward affair. It feels like being the only person in a shop with the entire focus of the bored sales force on you. I prefer the freedom to roam and kick things at will but we dutifully wandered from room to room mainly in silence. Occasionally Ms Realtor pointed out a feature – that's where the fridge goes. I'm not sure what she thought

I'd put in an empty rectangular-shaped hole in the kitchen wall – a coffin? The house felt cosy and appeared solid both inside and out. Not that I have a clue about anything structural: if I was intending to go further I would obtain a builder's report.

I discovered it was a 1920s house, and it had a dignified and stately feel. It was easily spacious enough for three and, vitally, it had a backyard big enough for growing vegetables and playing games. Many houses that I'd viewed were on recently subdivided sections and had little garden and sod all grass (excuse the awful pun). When you have smaller children, six and eight, the last thing you want is to have to take them to the park when they want to play outside, as I was doing currently.

When we completed the grand tour Ms Realtor politely inquired, 'When do you think your partner will be able to view the house?' The penny dropped. On my own with no wife, girlfriend, partner or significant other she thought I had the authority to do nothing. I was a mere scout. Ms Realtor clearly expected that she would have to repeat the tour when the real decision maker turned up. I know this sounds like stereotyping, but this must be what she encounters on a day-to-day basis. It seems the women are the decision makers and males go along to keep the peace. 'Anything for a quiet life,' my Dad was known to mutter, mainly under his breath.

When I related this story to Cathy she agreed instantly. Apparently the houses she'd been involved in purchasing had the 'correct' decision made before a male, her ex in this case, was even starting to contemplate the indoor-outdoor flow and where to position his drinks cabinet.

'Not any time soon,' I said. 'I'm separated.' I elected not to explain the international nature of my current situation as I thought it would only add confusion.

'I'm sorry to hear that.'

Yeah, right, I thought. Separations must be like fuel for the real-estate industry.

'Who are you using to sell your current home?'

'It's not being sold. My wife, ex-wife,' I corrected myself, 'is keeping it.' It seemed an innocent question but I realised that I was playing my cards poorly. She now knew I had cash. I'd inadvertently spilt some of my blood in the water.

'I see. It's a tough time, so much change. When I separated, it all got so messy.'

'I guess it's always tough,' I said. 'Can I see the master bedroom again?'

'Sure, follow me,' she said, slinking back into the house.

Okay that's not how the exchange finished at all, that's just me flexing my artistic licence. Probably inadvisably. This isn't, maybe unfortunately, the confessions of a single dad or real-estate agent. It would make an interesting variation on real-estate-based reality TV shows like *Escape to the Country*. It would certainly push up their ratings somewhat.

Back to the story.

The house was perfect and after a brief negotiation I agreed to buy at the house's rateable value which was in line with what houses were currently fetching. My blonde, well-dressed, attractive, single and now richer real-estate agent said I owed her a 'decent' bottle of wine for talking the seller down. I may have but, given the commission she just earned, the wine didn't happen.

So in November 2008, four months after I became single, Rog, Liv and I moved into the first house I had owned by myself. I completed all the necessary paperwork the school required and, as the children were now 'in zone', they were accepted for the upcoming year. Summer was knocking on the door, though it doesn't always turn up on time in Palmerston North. Everything seemed to be falling into place.

Reflections

- *If you're left with the money and not the house, don't make the mistake of thinking it will last forever. It won't.*
- *House hunting is difficult, so find a friend whose opinion you value to help. You'll get a valuable second opinion and, if you appear as a couple, it's likely you'll be taken more seriously.*
- *If you can, discuss the future schools your children might attend with your ex. House buying can be a strategic decision and being in the appropriate school zones can remove future stress.*
- *Maintain respectable working relationships with real-estate agents ...*

5. Muddling Through

Muddle through – to succeed in some undertaking in spite of lack of organisation.
Collins English Dictionary

I pride myself on being a big-picture person – someone who doesn't get lost in the detail. This is a valuable attribute in my working life, but I quickly learnt that it doesn't translate well to home life when there's no one to make sure everything's organised. In the weeks and months after my separation, my lack of attention to detail was highlighted to me on a regular basis.

Excursions with the children resulted in us getting to the venue with the children clothed in the required kit but with nothing else. Cold days at hockey: 'Sorry darling, I forgot to bring you a jacket. And some water.' Hot days at cricket: 'Sorry mate, I forgot to pack a hat and sunscreen. And some water.'

My road-to-Damascus moment came when I took Liv, six at the time, to hockey. I had Liv and her hockey stick and we were heading to Manawaroa Park on time. So far so good. Hockey, like many sports involving small children, is an all-in brawl. You can't see the hockey ball for enthusiastic bodies and wildly swinging sticks. Given the mayhem that takes place, the rule was, quite rightly: no mouthguard, no game.

In the car Liv sat silently chewing her gum. She wasn't her usual chatterbox self and I thought she may not be feeling well. But when we arrived she perked up, bolted out of the car and took off at a gallop to warm up with her team mates. I was left to carry her gear which, I discovered, wasn't that onerous as there was nothing to carry. Not even water.

It was an exciting game and Liv was, as usual, in the thick of the action. She managed to get her fair share of hits and the occasional kick, and triumphantly scored a goal. After the game, as we strolled back to the car, she was back to her chatty self.

'I whacked it hard, did you see?'

'You were awesome.'

'I'm thirsty.'

'I'll get you a drink on the way home. And hot chips,' I hastily added to sweeten the deal.

'Yay! I'm cold, where's my jacket?'

'The car's just over there. We'll get your boots off and you'll soon warm up inside.' I would like to think that this exchange was the origin of my awakening but I wasn't on the road to Damascus yet. Liv sat on the bumper chatting away about the game and her heroics while I took her boots off.

'Right, throw your stick in the boot and give me your mouthguard.'

Liv looked at me wide-eyed. 'I left my mouthguard at home.'

'No you didn't. You had it in during the game. I saw you were wearing it. Have you dropped it?' My voice became accusing.

'No it's at home. I used my bubble gum.'

Liv had played the entire game with her bubble gum stuck between her top lip and teeth to make it look as if she was wearing a mouthguard. I was quietly impressed with her resourcefulness and, as it's my responsibility to ensure she has everything she needs including her mouthguard, how could I be angry? I gave her a big hug and no more was said.

Later that evening when I relayed the story on the phone to Cathy. I considered it to be merely an amusing anecdote, so I expected her to burst out laughing. But instead I got a thorough dressing down for being a useless and careless parent. I was sternly reminded, over an extended period, how my forgetfulness could have resulted in Liv's teeth being knocked out – all of them apparently. 'How funny would that have been, hmmm?'

In the course of the conversation, as Cathy became less enraged, I discovered that her son had suffered damage to his teeth on a seesaw while under the relatively lazy and wandering eye of his father, hence the reaction. It was this conversation, and not the incident itself, that saw me take my first step towards Damascus.

TAKING CHARGE

The question that confronted me was – why was I hopeless at organising my children? On reflection, I think the following is what was happening. When you're in a relationship you become overly reliant on the strengths of your partner and end up taking those strengths for granted. Ensuring the children had everything they needed, and everything they could possibly need, was Rose's domain. She was brilliant at it.

An unfortunate side effect the arrival of children brings is the death of spontaneity, including travel. Driving off into the sunset on a whim was replaced by the need for Rose's military-style planning. Going anywhere involved an expedition-sized load of equipment: pram, cot, nappies, toys, a change of clothes, formula, sterilising unit, bibs, more clothes, dummies, food, water, yet more clothes, all sorts of creams, etc. On top of that there was the equally sizable pile of necessities that Rose required for herself.

It may be stereotyping but females seem to need more 'things' than males by a factor of about ten. Armed with my wallet and keys, I feel in a position to cope for a few days no matter where I ended up. A change of underwear is nice, but not essential. Really! I might add a toothbrush to the list but I could always sneak Rose's when she wasn't looking.

It was only after I'd packed the car, Tetris style, with the children's gear, Rose's gear and my toothbrush that Rog and Liv were allowed on board. If there was room. All that planning, packing, unpacking to check if various items had been packed and swearing tends to dampen excitement and increase tension. That isn't the ideal way to start a trip as the whole point of getting away is to reduce tension and increase excitement.

Cathy, I discovered, is also legendary at travel preparation which means her ex was probably as useless as I appear to be. When I visited her in England in the winter of 2010, she met me at Heathrow One as usual but I noticed she had unusually packed supplies of food, water, a radio, clothes for both of us, a shovel and sleeping bags.

'In case we get stuck on the M25,' she explained.

I was still jet lagged and I wondered if I had missed an ice age since leaving New Zealand. It seemed I had. The first clue I should have picked up on was the hour delay on the Heathrow tarmac. The plane couldn't cover the 400 metres from the runway to the terminal because snow had blanketed the ground and the pilots couldn't tell where the taxi-way was.

We drove a hundred or so metres onto the motorway before we encountered the first of what became many traffic jams. As we waited I didn't miss the second clue because it isn't every day you see a snow buggy cruising smoothly down the motorway.

In normal driving conditions it takes two hours to get to Canterbury from Heathrow, but that trip took nearly eight. If I'd been picking up Cathy, the only emergency supplies would be the mints I keep in the glove box.

Liv's hockey episode made it clear that I was currently finding domestic organisation a challenge and quick improvement was required. My period of delegating responsibility to the children was over. Their constant and consistent forgetfulness told me I was barking up the wrong tree. They were playing their part perfectly – carefree and happy-go-lucky children. It was me who was missing in action.

I took a leaf out of Cathy's book and bought a small bag for the car and stocked it with emergency essentials such as wipes, tissues, hair ties, band aids, paracetamol and, unsurprisingly, a bottle of water. This was basically a range of items that might be required when we were out and about or to cover forgetful indiscretions. I also started taking more time before we left the house, asking myself questions such as: what do we need? What could go wrong? What would Rose or Cathy take?

It isn't rocket science and my improvement was immediate. For sports, I made sure all the required kit plus food, drink, hat, sunscreen and whatever else may be required was packed. I was now able to stand tall and share knowing smiles with other like-minded parents when an ill-prepared parent was flapping about looking for a missing item. 'Do you need to borrow some sun cream,' I was able to helpfully, and smugly, offer.

To cover school I started checking with the children in the evening to see if anything special was required for the next day such as: money, equipment, forms completed or, heaven forbid, baking. Items required were then strategically positioned blocking the front door so we had to physically move them to leave the house.

Sadly it isn't a perfect system. I've watched Liv kick her togs out of the way so she could open the door. Sometimes, on my return home, I find the needed kit, book, money or lunch patiently waiting having been hoofed out of the way. Ninety-five per cent of the time it's Liv and the other time is usually Liv. With a resigned, but philosophical sigh, I stroll back to her classroom. I catch her eye and hold up the forgotten article and she charges over calling 'Daddyyyyy', which is payment enough.

I've continued to refine the way I organise and although I would like to think of myself as bloody organised, I'm probably still haphazard at best. After all, being well organised for a period of time just invites complacency. It's like disaster prepping: unless you're slightly neurotic, you drop your guard over time. After the tragic 2011 earthquake in Christchurch there was a sharp rise in the sale of torches, batteries and water containers. But, like my emergency car supplies, I bet they're all under a layer of dust and will be useless if, and when, they're needed. One day Rog wanted to wipe his hands when we were in the car. With a certain amount of pride, I reminded him of the emergency kit. The wipes were bone dry, stiff as cardboard and disintegrated on touch. Unfortunately, when it comes to emergency supplies, it's not the thought that counts!

I remain much better at keeping on top of the children's events and I feel that's more important than wiping hands. By way of example, as we were leaving the house for school, I had a sudden 'something's not quite right' feeling and halted the procession.

'Have we got everything?'

Rog and Liv stopped and assumed Homer-like poses, but I was far from reassured by their tentative and wholly unconfident reply of 'Aaaah, yep'.

'Are you sure?'

'Yes,' this time with eyes rolling and more than a hint of impatience.

'Okay,' I said reluctantly. 'Let's go.'

I couldn't put my finger on it and everything seemed to be in order: two children, two bags with books and lunches in appropriate school clothes. Three steps later and the 'Aha' moment arrived – it was the school clothes.

'Rog, isn't it mufti-day today?'

Wordlessly he spun around and headed back inside. He emerged a couple of minutes later in mufti, smiling. He brushed my shoulder as he wandered past, which I took as a twelve-year-old's equivalent of a pat on the back. I felt seven feet tall, organised, attentive, alert and generally 'da bomb'. Although life has a way of bringing you quickly back to reality.

BACK TO EARTH

Sam, my nanny at the time (and I cover the joy of having a nanny soon), picked up the children from school and looked after them until around six o'clock. In theory, homework was done, chores attended to and games played, but I gratefully settled for alive and happy! This worked flawlessly as Sam, and after her Brooke, were as reliable as Swiss watches.

It was, therefore, puzzling to arrive home not long after my mufti-day save and find the front door locked as Sam didn't usually do this. Thankfully in Palmerston North we don't feel under siege during the day. I let myself in and was met by a pensive-looking Liv and no Sam. Rog, I noticed, seemed wholly unconcerned and was engrossed in his computer. Liv told me that Sam didn't pick her or Rog up and that they walked home by themselves.

I was shocked and disappointed. The children were, however, fine. Living close to their schools meant it didn't take long to get home and use the emergency key which I'd installed for this situation. It also comes in useful when I walk to the pub and forget my keys, which I did twice before installing it. They then locked themselves in and remained holed up for two and half hours until I arrived home. Please don't paint this into a picture of two terrified and abandoned waifs. They had consoled themselves by eating biscuits and making a milkshake. They were fine.

I pondered what action to take. Sam was a fantastic nanny, but this was a major lapse. Even if she'd been in an emergency I would have expected her to contact me. It was about then the synapses in my brain started firing and dragged back my conversation with Sam the previous week.

'Remember I'm on holiday when you next have the children,' Sam said as she was about to leave.

'Yep, you've told me a couple of times.'

'I know but you're very busy at the moment.'

'Don't worry, I've got it covered.'

Oops. It's lucky I can't be sacked as Dad. Hand on heart, that's the first time since the children were born that I wasn't where I was supposed to be. And although they acted exactly as we'd planned, it was an admirable effort on their part all the same. The one aspect that hadn't worked as planned was they were meant to ring me on my mobile. Somehow Rog had rung the wrong number twice, leaving messages that must have bewildered some unfortunate person or caused them to go charging home only to discover they were on a wild goose chase.

All's well that ends well, but it's not a situation I plan to repeat. I now keep all the children's appointments, and who's picking them up, in my work diary and this has meant all events are in one place. There's been no recurrence, so far, and that shows that I *can* learn from my experiences, which is one of the important themes in this book.

There was no point swearing the children to secrecy. The next time we visited Grandma we were scarcely in the door before the story came blurting out. Thanks for that, blabber mouths.

Reflections

- *When you're a single dad you have to be organised. Being on top of things makes everyone's life easier.*
- *Children can be very resourceful, and this is to be encouraged, but let them develop this skill without an expensive trip to the dentist.*
- *Maintaining a supply of practical items in the car makes sense but you need to keep them refreshed. Five-year-old wipes don't work very well.*
- *Have emergency procedures for when things go awry and make sure your children understand them. Hiding a key that your children, and you, can use in emergencies is a great idea.*
- *Mistakes are opportunities to learn so don't beat yourself up if something goes wrong. You can beat yourself up if you repeat the mistake.*
- *Listen to your nanny closely.*

6. Childcare

If your kids are giving you a headache, follow the directions on the aspirin bottle, especially the part that says 'Keep away from children'.

Susan Savannah (author)

One of the first hurdles I encountered as a single dad was after-school care. Rose and I both needed to work, as literally overnight we'd both become SITCOMs – Single-Income Two Children Oppressive Mortgage. A work day that stopped around 2.30 to pick up the children wasn't going to work.

For after-school care Rose and I had used a friend and near neighbour, Susie, who had three boys of a similar age. She picked up all five children (rather her than me) from kindergarten and school and looked after them until 5pm. Their home was set up for children and they loved pets. In fact they had three Rhodesian Ridgebacks, each of which took up the same space as a person. It was slightly unnerving to see my diminutive little ones stretching up to pat a dog that must have thought they resembled chew toys. Nothing untoward ever happened and the dogs were well cared for and well behaved.

The only trouble we experienced concerned Thursday nights for about two months. During this time, and only on Thursdays, peace on earth did not have a hope in our house until Friday, around 3am. The culprit was Liv, who was two at the time. Every night except Thursdays we popped her down and she gently fell asleep like the angel she resembled. But on Thursday nights it was pandemonium. Not only wouldn't she sleep but she howled and screamed, unnervingly resembling Linda Blair in *The Exorcist*.

The first time this happened Rose and I acted like the responsible parents we are. One of us would pick her up and gently calm her until the alarming shade of scarlet drained from her face. Once settled, we would tuck her back into her cot and sneak out the door. This worked a treat most nights but not on Thursdays, when she would resume her howling with renewed vigour. I couldn't help but be impressed with the wee mite's stamina and vocal power.

We checked everything: nappy, thirsty, hot, cold. We tried everything we knew. Nothing worked. The only course of action left was to shut the doors between her and us and wait her out. No baby monitor was required. In the next room, Rog thankfully slept through these episodes oblivious to his sister's predicament. Goodness knows what the neighbours thought. In the suburbs you generally knew how well your neighbours were getting on and, uncomfortably, how often.

One Thursday Liv was protesting loudly and vehemently as usual while I ignored her in the lounge. In amongst the usual noise I heard a large thump, which seemed to be the movie-esque sound of a body hitting carpet. I listened intently but the usual cacophony had been replaced with silence. I raced in and found Liv, wide-eyed, lying on her back on her bedroom floor. We stared at each other and I don't know who was more surprised. Liv, standing on her tip toes, could only just reach the top of her cot. She would look like the cartoon figure Chad staring over a wall.

I picked her up and sat on the floor cuddling her. I was amazed at the effort that must have been required to haul herself out of her cot. It was obviously possible, but before that moment I would have bet against it substantially. I'm not sure how long we sat there, but eventually she drifted off to sleep. With a long drawn-out yawn (from me that is), I popped her back in her cot and ever so gently tucked her in as though she was unstable explosives. She lay there, peaceful and asleep. I left her room on tip toes and shut the door with the lightest of clicks.

I got two steps into the lounge when the howling started once more.

Rose and I naturally asked Susie what she did on Thursdays. We thought it must be sugar, food colouring or something different in Liv's day such as back-to-back horror movies. But apart from being taken grocery shopping, Susie did nothing out of the ordinary. We were at a loss as to what to do when, as suddenly as it started, it stopped. I was thankful it was over and put it into the mysterious happenings category with the grassy knoll, Harold Holt and Roswell.

NANNIES

Let's return to the issue of after-school care. As Rose and I were changing the children's school we also needed to organise new after-school care. Unfortunately, the existing arrangements with Susie wouldn't work logistically. It wasn't lost on me that in addition to any anxiety the children were feeling as a result of the separation, we were adding a new school and new after-school care. In hindsight it looks as if we were stress testing our children's resilience. But while there were issues, there proved to be nothing major or lasting – thankfully, or maybe luckily.

The new school year was rapidly approaching and we needed to get something organised. Through a friend of a friend Rose and I met Megan who, along with her husband and two children, had recently emigrated from Zimbabwe. Megan was a French teacher with a degree in law but they had only been in New Zealand for a few months and she wasn't keen on diving back into full-time work immediately. They were warm and friendly with a wonderfully eclectic house and over coffee we organised for Megan to pick up our two when she picked up her two and look after them until 5pm.

This arrangement was perfect for me as Megan lived only a short walk away, which made picking up the children easy. It didn't work as well for Rose, though, and halfway through the school year she decided to change and get her mother to provide the after-school care. Using my ex-mother-in-law was not an attractive option and so I continued with Megan. My relationship with Rose's mother thawed over the years but back then it was, in polite language, frosty.

Although using Megan worked well for me, when Rose changed it also changed some of the subtleties of the arrangement for the children. It became clear that for the children to thrive when they were with me I needed help based at my house. They were still finding their feet in amongst all the change and, even being in a house as lovely as Megan's, it wasn't their own home. I felt that's what they required. I needed a nanny.

The male and female concepts of a nanny appear to be different, causing nannies to have acquired a reputation, unjustified no doubt, of being dangerous to relationships. Years earlier Rose and I had considered hiring a nanny and she had talked about having a male one for that precise reason. The thought of a male nanny seemed wrong to me even though conceptually there should be no difference. Cathy had similar stories and thoughts in relation to nannies. During her marriage her husband was, it seemed, over-keen to hire 'pretty' nannies and happy to overlook any shortcomings in their credentials – such as an absence of childcare experience.

Despite this urban myth that males can't be trusted around nannies, my motivation for hiring a nanny was genuine and there was no cause for concern. All I was interested in was someone reliable who was great with children. Being easy on the eye wasn't a requirement.

I placed an ad in the local *Student Job Search* website. My logic was that female students looking for work as nannies should be reliable and would be keen for the work – or, more accurately, the money. I checked the other ads and most people were offering $15 an hour, so I offered $17.50 an hour. This propelled my ad to the top in terms of financial attractiveness. It doesn't take much to make a difference and at three hours a day every second week, the extra $2.50 an hour wasn't going to break my bank.

Three people expressed interest immediately but it was Sam's CV that stood out. A second-year accounting student (I normally dislike accountants on principle), she had previously nannied for a former colleague who lived in Whanganui. A quick email confirmed Sam was lovely, reliable and extremely capable. The deal was sealed by the line in my former colleague's email – *But please don't employ her, as I don't want to lose her.* Sorry, but my rate was higher and when it comes to money size definitely matters!

Sam was as good as her CV looked and she nannied for me for three years. As soon as I enjoyed the benefits of a nanny I could scarcely comprehend how I'd coped before. She looked after the children until 6pm during the week, allowing me a full work day. This let me keep my sanity and, most importantly, it worked brilliantly for the children. They could come home and flop on the couch, watch TV, raid the fridge or, as a last resort, do their homework. All in the comfort of their own home.

Sam supported by her friend Haley and then Brooke were wonderful nannies. Maybe I've been lucky to have had such kind and responsible nannies. Though I was paying slightly more, which allowed a better choice, you still probably need luck when hiring twenty-year-olds. I think choosing students is a sound strategy as they tend to be people with drive and ambition.

FAMILY

For many recently separated parents the additional expense of a nanny may be prohibitive. If you're in this situation then being able to call upon friends and family may allow you to develop a similar arrangement. I would encourage the odd bottle of wine or box of chocolates to say thank you in the absence of cash.

In my case it was my mum who was an invaluable component in my childcare arrangements. Having a family member able and, crucially, willing to look after the children is a godsend. Without her availability, often at short notice, work, study and fitness (and sometimes the pub) would have all been much harder to coordinate. It must run in my family as I remember that as a child if I was at home sick, my grandma (my mum's mum) would come over to do the washing. She'd then come back in the afternoon to bring it in and fold it. 'Just in case it rained,' she would tell me as she brought in orange juice and biscuits.

On Monday evenings I normally drop Rog and Liv off at Grandma's for dinner and I head off to karate or the gym. When I return, shattered and sweaty, I find happy, well-fed children and a takeaway home-cooked meal. It doesn't get better than that. Close though is pizza night on Friday. My mum comes over and orders pizza, allowing me to carry on working, studying or hitting the gym. I drop her back home and then tuck into the leftover pizza. And as by Friday I feel I've earned it, the *odd* beer goes well with pizza. That's one, three …

It isn't only after-school that needs to be organised with military precision. Mornings can also be a challenge. To run my business I sometimes have to be on the road early. For a number of years I had a client based in Dannevirke, about an hour away by car, who scheduled a weekly 7.30am breakfast meeting. I was able to attend because my mum would arrive at 6.15am, leaving me free to disappear before the children were awake. I made sure everything was organised – breakfast was laid out, school lunches were made, school bags were packed and a cup of tea poured. That left my mum to have fun, supervise teeth cleaning and wander with them to school, which she loved doing.

This worked almost flawlessly but I hadn't factored in the mischievous child element. After three meetings in a row there was a voice message waiting from my mum. One or other of my dear children, probably decided by scissors, stone and paper, didn't feel well and as Mum couldn't walk one and leave the other home alone, they were both off sick for the day. I would arrive home to find one child trying to look poorly but failing dismally and the other looking like the cat that had got the cream. Clever ratbags. The children and I had a 'chat' about this state of affairs and it never happened again.

The help Mum gives me is even more indispensable when the children are legitimately sick. I'm certain parents, not just single parents, understand the total disregard children have for well-constructed plans through their thoughtless and untimely sicknesses. It throws the world into chaos. On the occasions my mum isn't available, I usually resort to heading into work armed with toys and chocolate muffins with my sick child in tow. I hide them in an unused office, promise it won't be long and cross my fingers. This tactic usually buys me an hour or two, which is often all I need to get the day back under control.

All the childcare measures that I have in put in place have made life smoother for everyone. I empathise with single parents who have no family support and have to do everything. It must be a limiting situation. As a single dad, having a responsible nanny and a supportive mum has made the world of difference to what I am able to achieve and to the children's happiness. Without this support maybe I would have lowered my expectations or drunk more and got bitter and twisted. I'm glad I haven't had to find out!

Reflections

- *If you can afford to hire a nanny, do it. You'll be astounded at the difference a nanny can make to your life. Targeting university students makes sense.*
- *It's often said that you get what you pay for and paying a little more than the competition will result in a happy nanny who wants to keep the job. It also feels good to help someone along their educational journey.*
- *Having the same after-school care in both houses is ideal. Whatever the arrangements, make sure they work for your children, not only for you.*
- *Family support makes life much easier. If you don't have family available, try buddying up with other single parents.*
- *Make things as pleasant and easy as possible for whoever is looking after your children, especially family members. The odd box of chocolates or bottle of wine goes a long way.*
- *Never underestimate your children's ability to work whatever care arrangements you establish to their own advantage.*

7. Fashion

Fashion is what you adopt when you don't know who you are.
Quentin Crisp (writer and performer, 1908-99)

Clothes provide a range of issues for the fashion-semi-conscious single dad. It stung me when I read Josh Wolf, the author of *It Takes Balls*, referring to men who have let their wardrobe decline leaving one going-out shirt. I'm not that bad but there have also been times when I wasn't far off. His comments weren't a direct hit, but they were a decent glancing blow and wake-up call.

Making sure you're presentable should be a priority but you also have to consider your children. Until they wrestle the responsibility off you, which can be anywhere between ages five and eighteen, what they wear is down to you. I'm not sure what other parents do but in the absence of a helping feminine eye I have adopted a relaxed policy aligned to the French term of laissez-faire. Basically I let the children choose. This has resulted in some interesting selections but so far I haven't had to make them change apart from insisting that more or less clothing be worn depending on the weather.

My strategy is that the children will develop good judgement over time. It may sound like I'm abdicating responsibility, but when you consider the alternative – that I lay out their clothes each day – I think letting the children choose makes a lot more sense. Especially in the long term.

Although I haven't overturned a clothing choice I have needed to ask a few searching questions on occasions.

'Does that top really go with those shorts?'

'Do you think those trousers are a bit short for you now?'

'Are jandals appropriate when there's a frost?'

The children's answer to these questions is normally a clipped 'Yes' and I have invariably gone with the flow, though Liv's love of jandals almost forced my hand. Jandals (it's slang for 'Japanese sandals') is the New Zealand equivalent of thongs in Australia, slops in South Africa and flip-flops in the UK. Liv briefly acquired the nickname 'Jandals' at school because she wore them exclusively for a year, without major illness I hasten to add. Fortunately we don't live in Australia – 'Thongs' would be an embarrassing nickname.

Does this mean Rog and Liv *have* developed a sharp fashion sense? Well, yes and no and – as they will read this one day – I won't say who's the yes and who's the no. One of them was observed recently, ready to go out to dinner, with their pants on back to front. That example, while hilarious, is unrepresentative and normally they're pretty sharp. In fact I've noticed as they've approached their teen years that they've become more conscious of their appearance and upped their game accordingly. If they've made a considerable effort I politely inquire about a boyfriend or girlfriend and get attacked for my curiosity.

The arrival of a school uniform made school mornings easier for Rog as it eliminated choice. It wasn't a massive change for him as, like many boys, he expended little time on such decisions. Liv, on the other hand, dreaded the arrival of a school uniform as she was forced to wear a skirt. Before this, the last time I remembered Liv in anything resembling a skirt was for a family event when she was four. She had looked cute in her white one-piece party dress, though she hadn't been overly impressed. I have a charming family photo with

Rose, Rog and I beaming at the camera — but all we can see of Liv is her back. The introduction of shoes also caused Liv distress. The choice was Roman sandals or solid, sensible black shoes. No jandals.

SKIN IN THE GAME

Buying clothes for children is a task I don't relish. Rose, thankfully, is excellent at this though I sense her motivation is partly a fear of what I may choose. It's a legitimate fear but it works for me. The times I have been involved in buying clothes for the children I embark on hit-and-run raids. The children and I identify what we're buying, plan an attack picking out the stores in question, and we're in and out in record time. This approach can come unstuck. I once found myself at home with two left shoes, but who checks for that?

Rog loves my hit-and-run approach to shopping. There may be something in the male psyche that makes the thought of shopping expeditions abhorrent. In Rog's case it may be due to being subjected to shopping trips with Rose, Liv and various aunties, cousins and nieces. I empathise. I've stood — or sat when the shop is insightful enough to realise that keeping the male partner happy has a direct correlation with sales — with nothing to do except wander the store trying not to be observed hanging around the lingerie section. Come to think of it, I've never been taken on a lingerie shopping expedition. That's like shopping for meat and veges and ignoring the desserts isle. Moving on.

I'm not sure why males are wanted on clothes shopping trips. The answer to the inevitable question 'Does this look good on me?' is yes. That's after a suitable pause to give the impression I'm giving the question my full consideration. This is because I'm ready to leave. It makes no difference how long we've been there, I'm ready to leave and I'm sure I'm not alone. It's accepted wisdom that a male's opinion on clothes isn't highly valued so why bother to ask? I've come to the conclusion it's a test. It has to do with commitment and being a priority over whatever else we want to be doing, such as watching sport. Technology has come to our rescue via smartphones and now I can play Angry Birds or watch sport while I patiently wait.

Although I can't offer advice on selecting clothes, I can pass on a tip that works brilliantly with the children when you're buying clothes. Liv, ten at the time, was the first casualty of this approach when she needed new swimming togs after leaving hers in the changing rooms.

In my hit-and-run style, we attacked the local Rebel Sports store. I found the same brand and style as the togs she'd lost and, even better, they were half price at $25. It looked like my lucky day.

'Here you go, Liv,' I said as I handed them to her. 'Go and make sure they fit.'

'Okay,' she said, taking them but she made no move towards the changing rooms. Instead she carried on browsing through the rack of togs. This wasn't part of the plan but I waited patiently. My gaze intensified when she casually selected another pair of togs.

'These look cool,' she said and skipped off to the changing rooms.

I checked the price on a similar pair – $50. Hmmm.

It wasn't long, although it feels long when you're loitering around changing rooms, before Liv was back.

'Do they fit?' I asked

'Yep they both fit.'

'*Both?*'

'Please Daddy, can I have these ones?' she implored, holding up the expensive togs.

Girls have an innate ability to wrap their dads around their little finger. Unfortunately for Liv my days of guilt, when she and Rog could have anything as long as they were happy, were well behind me.

'What's wrong with these ones?' I asked, holding up the replacement togs. 'They're exactly what you had and they're half the price.'

'They're okay. But these are way cool. *Pleeeease*, Daddy.'

I paused. Normally I'd roll over in a situation like this as the money in question wasn't huge. But in a moment of inspiration I had an idea.

Holding up my preferred option I said, 'Here's the deal. You want the *cool* ones but these are fine and half the price, so I'll give you a choice. I'll happily pay for these ones but if you want the *cool* ones I'll pay the first $25, which is what I would be paying anyway, and the rest can come from your savings.' Liv had built an impressive bank balance from saving her chore money.

'What?' said Liv, looking astonished. Normally she was confronted with a simple choice and she either got what she wanted or she didn't. Thankfully she doesn't get moody when she doesn't get her way. Not yet anyway. But here she was faced with a third option and it involved unlocking some of her financial stockpile.

'You don't *need* the cool togs,' I explained, 'but if you really *want* them then you have to spend some of your own money. It's that simple.'

Rog, who'd been loitering without intent, ambled over suddenly interested in events. Although I'm sure he was enjoying his sister's predicament as only a sibling can, he knew that this would apply to him at some stage and it was in his best interests to understand the rules.

Liv silently weighed up her options. I didn't know which way she would go but, to her credit, she chose the cool togs. It was a win-win-win. Liv got the togs she wanted, I spent what I considered reasonable. The other major win, which didn't occur to me at the time, was that with her own money in the purchase, I didn't think that she'd lose them this time. And she didn't. She wore them until they started giving her a decent wedgie, not a good look!

It was a stroke of genius. I then went one step further to consolidate my gains. To thwart the children from just asking Rose to buy what they wanted, meaning I'd pay half as that is how we settle costs relating to the children, I told Rose the story. She thought it was a great idea. Sorry guys but that's checkmate.

Rose and I have both used this approach in a range of situations and it has worked a treat. When Rog started high school I bought him a house key in case he got home before me or in the event of an emergency. Knowing Rog, as a boy, would lose it immediately I made him a deal: if he loses the key he has to pay for the replacement *and* the lost key. So it's free as long as he doesn't lose it. (He hasn't.)

As for Liv, she went halves on a pair of tennis-ball-green shoes that she wanted but didn't need. Those are the first shoes I've ever seen her clean, although she did use Grandma's face cloth for the task. Progress of sorts.

STAYING HIP

Buying clothes for myself I also find a struggle. It isn't the task itself, which is pretty straightforward, it's the selection of clothes without experiencing buyer's remorse. To mitigate this I've found that a woman's opinion is invaluable and has saved me from wasting money on dubious clothes I'm unlikely to wear. Rose and Cathy were both blessed with brutal honesty, which is what is needed. Feedback such as 'Those trousers make you look like you're advertising your private parts' makes decision making easy. After all, they had a vested interest in making sure I looked presentable if not gorgeous because they had to stand next to me.

Being single, without that critical feminine eye, has meant my clothes buying has become infrequent, allowing me to slide towards owning only one respectable shirt.

There are other signs that tell me that it's time to invest in new clothes. It's when I feel each undulation in the footpath through the wafer-thin soles of my shoes. My jeans lose that jeans feel and although they're still wearable, it's obvious they should be retired. Favourite shirts deserve a commendation for the service able to be wrung from them. I have even resorted to using sticky tape to repair the cuffs of my real favourites. On the inside that is, and out of sight.

It keeps them looking respectable from a distance and I figure if anyone is close enough to see the inside of my cuffs then the tape has done its job.

Replacing items such as jeans is relatively straightforward. Unless I've put on weight, or height, I just the buy same style, that's a pair of 503s with a 33 waist and 34 leg. I try them on but it's a precaution and not a fashion check. Shoes, UK size 10, socks and underwear are also easy to replace and hard to get wrong and I love the feel of new cushion-soled gym socks. They're one item of clothing that I buy with a genuine sense of delight.

When Cathy and I were together I usually took the opportunity to employ her feminine eye and buy clothes when I was visiting her in England. There the range of clothes is massive compared to Palmerston North. There are malls so large that they have more than one of the same store! I took the children to one called Bluewater and kept a watchful eye on them — if I lost them, they could end up in another district.

Cathy also sent clothes over when she found items that she thought would suit me. She was almost never wrong, though the metrosexual pink shirt has still to make its debut. It does feel good to say 'It's a Ted Baker from London', although I'm sure that type of comment creates mixed impressions ranging from 'tosser' to 'big tosser'.

While writing this chapter I decided to check out the status of the children's and my wardrobes and drawers. I found that the children are carting clothes between houses that they will never wear. Some clearly haven't fitted them in years.

I also discovered that I have clothes that have been on hangers so long that the shoulders are permanently hanger-shaped. In fact of the roughly fifty items in my wardrobe I cycle through only about ten of them. I didn't, however, have a cleanout as I probably should have. Part of me is confident that some of my older clothes will be trendy again. One day even flares will be back.

Overall I think I need to be more up to date. I'm *okay*, but the slippery slope isn't far away and I refuse to look like many men my age who have clearly given up – given up on caring about what they look like, about other people's opinions and any chance of a feminine double take. Certainly the last thing I want is Liv to start taking a motherly role when it comes to *my* dress sense ...

'Dad, you're not wearing that shirt with those trousers, are you?'

Reflections

- Don't let your wardrobe decline into embarrassment for your sake and your children's.
- Letting your children pick the clothes they want to wear works in the long run. Patience and fashion-blindness is required, though.
- Being confident and competent to buy clothes for your children is desirable. Don't abdicate the task even if you have a significant other with exceptional fashion sense.
- Get your children to have a financial stake in their purchases whenever possible. This fundamentally changes the way they value and care for those items.
- When you're buying clothes for yourself take someone with you whose taste you trust. This will help avoid buyer's remorse or looking odd.
- Never allow your daughter to assume the role of your fashion advisor. Unless, of course, she's over twenty and a fashion designer. Then listen carefully and do what you're told.

8. The F Word, Alright?

Life is too short to stuff a mushroom.
Storm Jameson (journalist and author, 1891-1986)

Cooking has a polarising effect on people. You either love it or you see it as a chore. As a single dad I've grown to dislike it, though I'd stop short of saying I hate it. Cooking is required to keep my children alive and somewhat quiet as they tend to become fixated with food when they're hungry.

I can't remember disliking cooking with the same intensity when I was married. Rose and I would regularly cook together and when the children were tiny and finding time to go out for dinner was hard, we had dinner parties at home for just us. One of us would cook the entrée and dessert and the other the main. It's possibly the absence of adult company, coupled with Rog and Liv's fondness for plain food, that makes cooking a chore far closer to doing the washing than a pleasure.

Rog is more adventurous with food but Liv, until recently that is, is a food bore. I find this strange as she loves cooking programmes with their extravagant food spectacles. Place anything actually resembling this in front of her and wait for the look of disbelief. You end up cooking for the lowest common denominator, in my case Liv. And so we end up eating unexciting food. Thankfully she's starting to change as her tastes develop; relatively innocuous dishes like butter chicken are now gracing our table.

I prefer food that requires minimal handling, like roasts. Turn on the oven, put the roast in oven and go watch TV. Perfect. One evening, however, early in my life as a single dad, I decided to be adventurous and cook something fancy. I can't remember what it was except that it contained chicken and a range of spices I had to buy. It took planning and preparation, not to mention the time actually cooking. Surprisingly, it was really good, even if I do say so myself. I plated it nicely (I used that phrase only to show that cooking shows are like passive smoking) and we sat down to my version of *Come Dine With Me*. 'Bon appetit, les enfants.' They looked at it, picked at it and pushed it around the plate. I encouraged them to give it a try but they were having none of it. So I buttered a stack of bread and they were happy. My days of cooking haute cuisine were over. The majority of the spices were never used again and were thrown out years later when I saw their best-before dates. In my naivety I hadn't thought spices would go off.

I know people such as Cathy and Uri (a university colleague) who counter the differing tastes of their family by cooking, apparently happily, different meals for everyone. That should be illegal. It would be like splitting the washing based on whose clothes they were. It's hard enough for me to be bothered with the whites-and-coloured palaver – which I thought was an urban myth until the children ended up with pink sheets. I told them they were new and, as they like new stuff, they were pleased. You have to think on your feet to stay one step ahead of your children.

For evening meals when I have the children my first task when I arrive home and I'm greeted by a hungry deputation is to deftly sidestep them and grab a cold beer. That's after my nanny has gone – must keep up appearances. Then I start working out what to rustle up for dinner. Typically I haven't thought much about it until then, which is why we are well known at a number of local restaurants. I've improved over the years but I'm miles away from the apparent gold standard, which is shopping with a meal plan for the week. That makes me feel tired.

I think food expectations have risen in recent years thanks to the plethora of cooking shows now on. There are chefs of all shapes, sizes and tastes whipping up exotic and fancy dishes while the audience sit salivating Pavlov-like. Meanwhile I'm cooking pasta, opening the sauce and buttering bread. You can't live up to the standard that others have set. It's like taking your date to a body-building competition. Madness. Let him or her watch *Australia's Biggest Loser* and they'll look at you with renewed delight.

Then there's the implausibility of cooking shows which I thought were meant to be part of the reality TV genre. I'll pick on Jamie Oliver's show *15-Minute Meals*. The fifteen minutes doesn't include the time Jamie spends wandering around the farmers' market. Nor does it include the years required to assemble a kitchen stocked with every condiment and implement known to mankind. Fifteen minutes? Reality? Yeah, right.

My life and kitchen aren't like that. I admit it would be nice to open the fridge and grab chives, leeks, lemongrass (I'm not sure that even goes in the fridge), gluten and acid-free cherry tomatoes and freshly filleted orange roughy. That indicates a level of planning that I don't possess. I stock the fridge on a Sunday with a varied range of items and then work it out on the night. Items that don't get used quickly tend to linger. Leeks, for example, when they are rediscovered after a week or two look similar to flaccid spring onions.

My claim to fame in the kitchen is my talent for juggling eggs. The first time I demonstrated this skill to the children they were equally terrified and amazed at the risk involved. I juggled for about eight seconds before one got away and splatted, as eggs do when they hit the ground. Rog and Liv both stared open-mouthed. I thought it wasn't a bad effort considering I hadn't juggled in years and then it was with cricket balls. I was inspired to have another crack, excuse the pun, and I went to get another egg but I was thwarted by the members of my audience who leapt to the eggs' defence.

KEEPING OUT OF THE KITCHEN

The alternatives to home-cooked meals all have drawbacks. I refuse to raise my children on junk food. So we watched *Supersize Me* and *The Men that Made Us Fat* together so I could educate them on the perils of a junk-food diet. The look on their faces when Morgan Spurlock vomited his lunchtime quarter-pounder and fries out the car window was priceless. That scene has saved me hundreds of dollars and given my two a healthier future. Thanks for your sacrifice, Morgan, as that clearly wasn't trick photography.

We aren't saints, however. I do buy takeaways, and Friday has become known as pizza night. I try to keep junk food purchases to once a week but it isn't a hard and fast rule. We once had pizza three nights in succession – some weeks can be tough as a single parent, or any parent for that matter. The children thought it was great but I felt as if I was failing as a parent (though I struggle to put pizza and Indian takeaways in the same category as the multinational burger chains. That would be like calling alcohol a drug).

Restaurants are an option but that is no more than once a week at most as it's an expensive method of avoiding the kitchen. It wouldn't be as costly if the children and I didn't have drinks, entrées and desserts, but once I'm in a restaurant I'm resigned to the cost. A bonus is that we sit at a table and interact. It's not that we never sit at our dining table at home, but it's often simpler to plonk down on the couch and watch TV. The *News* or *America's Favourite Home Disasters That People Filmed When They Should Have Been Intervening*, depending on who finds the remote. I prefer that we sit at the table as I get to hear what's going on in the children's world. I have them captured for a whole fifteen minutes.

Takeaways and restaurants aren't the only options at the disposal of the thinking single dad who wants to avoid cooking. I've developed some routines that I judge as win-win, but I know it's the children and I who are the major beneficiaries. In particular on Monday evenings we visit my mum who loves having us over for dinner. Honestly, she does and the children love the roasts she cooks with vegetables and lashings of gravy.

Between pizza night, Monday at Mum's and one night dining out, I've covered three nights without having to set foot in the kitchen. Not bad. In a moment of inspiration I trimmed two more nights in a win-win-win arrangement with the children. I increased their chore-money on the proviso that they cook one evening meal and organise one breakfast each week. They win because they get cash, and I win for obvious reasons. It took a while for me to get the full benefit as they needed my help in the kitchen, but it was still a win because cooking with the children is fun. The third group of yet to be identified winners are their future flatmates and partners. Each year Rog and Liv will have cooked twenty-six meals and by the time they leave home they'll have a solid culinary repertoire. Rog tests this logic because he always wants to make tacos. Still, I've had far worse meals than tacos in my student days and they're fairly healthy.

Combining meals is a favoured weekend tactic of mine that lessens kitchen time. If I can withstand the complaints or the children sleep in, which they do more now, I can skip breakfast and we can have brunch. I do hear the odd rumble that they're being ripped off a meal. The rumblings threatened to escalate into open revolt when I invented 'brunchner', which is breakfast, lunch and dinner, and 'dinnerfast', dinner and breakfast. I've yet to have the courage to implement these.

MEALS FOR ONE

When the children are with me food provides an almost audible beat that keeps life moving. The pantry and fridge must be stocked and meals whisked up at a reasonable time if you want the world to spin smoothly. Without the children and their entreating, cajoling and nagging, there's no such impetus and consequently my kitchen rapidly resembles a hotel room containing coffee, tea, alcohol, chips and chocolate. I'm exaggerating slightly, it's not too bad at the start of the week.

I do find cooking for one is wholly uninspiring but, that said, I try and cook a couple of times a week to keep the bills down and my health up. I aim for quick and easy meals as I see no point in trying to prepare an intricate meal when I'm most likely to be watching the *News*. So it's tried and true meals like steak and salad, burger and chips or sometimes a roast if there's compelling sport on TV.

On rare occasions I try to be creative. On my way home one Friday after a few convivial drinks, I caught the distinctive and delicious smell of curry. Homer-like – Homer Simpson that is – my brain said 'Hmmm, curried sausages' and so I stopped at the supermarket and purchased the required ingredients. I knew the dish wasn't complex or time consuming and I soon settled down on the couch with a heaped plate of curried sausages and rice. They looked fantastic, although they weren't as yellow as I remembered.

One bite had me reaching for a drink to wash away the taste.

I'd made mustard sausages, not curried ones.

In my defence the tins and powders do look similar. I was gutted, though it highlighted the dangers of trying to follow a recipe post-beer. I wandered down to the local Indian takeaways for a real curry as Tiger, my late cat, tucked into the sausages. He died of old age – not the sausages.

On solo nights when I decide to shun the kitchen I buy what I consider to be healthy takeaways such as a kebab or Indian. I also drop into my mum's on an ad-hoc basis where my side of the conversation goes something like:

'Hi Mum.'

'Only if you've got enough.'

'Are you sure?'

'Is there any beer in the fridge?'

As Liv has grown she has sweetly taken to helping me in my solo weeks. She likes cooking on Sunday night and makes a big dish of lasagne or macaroni cheese ensuring I have leftovers for at least two nights, sometimes three. It's very thoughtful and it has shown me how much children can be in tune with the subtleties of the world around them.

One Sunday, as I was packing the car in preparation to drop the children off, Liv, who was around ten, suddenly became tearful. I had no idea why and so I sat with her and we chatted. What emerged was quite lovely. Because I was going to be by myself for the week she thought that I'd be sad and lonely. In my usual dad style, I assured her that dropping off her and Rog for the week was a joyous event. It wasn't long after this that Liv started cooking the big Sunday meals.

One aspect that is noticeable when the children are absent is that the standards of hygiene in the kitchen are significantly lowered. With the children around I keep the kitchen spotless so they don't see it as a place where they can dump and run. Without them leftovers, dishes and food packaging pile up on the bench and in the sink. Plates and cutlery are reused with a cursory wipe of the dishcloth. The odd food item will have been left out overnight to become a simple, quick breakfast. Anyway, I think it's a crime to waste good pizza.

The lengths to which my standards can be lowered was highlighted to me by a stuffed potato. I'd bought it on the way home after the gym and heated it in the microwave. As I was transferring it to a waiting plate – lined with salad I may add – the paper on which it was sitting ripped and it literally splatted on the kitchen floor. I was devastated. It was late, I was tired, I was hungry and the cupboards were bare. Now, there's no way in the world I would allow the children to eat anything that had hit the kitchen floor in that manner, but …

I think cooking and eating are activities that are at their finest when there are other adults involved. When you're single, with or without children, it's harder to find the motivation to aim for haute cuisine. Maybe there's a market for a reality TV programme focused on cooking for one. It would suit an alcoholic chef with only average standards and there must a few of them around.

I'm definitely in Storm's camp though. Life is too short to stuff a mushroom.

Reflections

- *When cooking for children, serve food they're likely to eat the vast majority of the time. It saves you crying into your penne all'arrabbiata.*
- *Real life and cooking shows are mutually exclusive. It's all down to smoke, mirrors and about twenty assistants.*
- *Educating your children on the dangers of a poor diet will save you money and will improve everyone's future health.*
- *Teaching children to cook will get you out of the kitchen and, if you insist on variety, arm them with a repertoire for their future.*
- *Cooking and eating alone isn't often fun. Aim for quick, easy and healthy.*
- *Have a dinner plan B when cooking after a few drinks.*

9. Domesticity

The cruel irony of housework: people only notice when you don't do it.
Danielle Raine (writer)

A single parent's chores seem endless. There's always a long, cyclical list of domestic duties waiting. I'm sure it's the same for parents in general, especially where one parent shoulders the domestic workload. And, let's be honest, it's usually the mother, despite her working arrangements. It may not be politically correct to say, but it's usually viewed as woman's work. Wrongly! It's thankless, unnoticed and mostly unrewarding work. I say 'mostly' as I find the result of vacuuming rather pleasing. That aside, as tasks they rank below cooking and above jamming my finger in the door. Just.

In the absence of the ability to delegate, keeping the house clean is difficult on two fronts. First, there's when the children are with me. They have an amazing capacity to make everything messy. It's an innate gift that they'll lose when they have children of their own. Some children, mostly boys I'm disappointed to say, never lose this ability and usually elect to marry their way into a tidier environment. They should come with warnings.

Second, there's when I am on my own. Then I can't be bothered cleaning as usually there's no one but me to benefit. The chapter on single dads and friends will give you a better understanding why my chances of unexpected visitors are remote, allowing laxness to reign.

THE CHILDREN ARE IN DA HOUSE

Let's take the weeks with the children first. There is nothing that they touch that stays clean or tidy. You name it: shoes, clothes, their rooms, the coffee table, the kitchen, their desks, the floor, not to mention the bathroom and toilet. It defies logic that they can make a mess with soap and toothpaste – two products whose sole purpose is to make things cleaner!

Food, in particular, can be slopped, spilled, dropped, dribbled and left anywhere. Frequently I find freshly and hurriedly wiped spills on the carpet or table. The giveaway is that it's a child's attempt to clean the minor disaster and it's a lacklustre effort at best. It's no wonder that pets love children. They are walking food distributors. Cathy recounted a story in which she'd brought a brand-new couch. On the first day it was in the house, her daughter let a fried egg slide off her plate and onto the armrest. All Cathy was able to say was 'I can't believe you did that!'

That's the way the world turns when children are in the house. I have given up on the concept of a stain-free carpet. There's no point in having such a lofty goal. Go into any house and you can work out how many children live there, and their ages, by a quick glance at the carpet in front of the TV and heaters. You don't need to be Sherlock Holmes.

> 'Two, I think you'll find, Watson. A boy and, if I'm not mistaken, a girl who has an aversion to vegetables. One or both are missing fingers or suffering from a malady that causes a severe shaking of the limbs. That or a tribe of African green monkeys have moved in. It could be either.'

I beg, threaten and, more recently, incentivise – but it appears to be impossible for Rog or Liv to keep areas clean and tidy. I wouldn't mind if the mess was contained in their rooms, but they invade as many spaces as possible. When they were little we did what all parents do: we followed them from room to room, cleaning up in their wake. Each morning they woke to an environment that was clean and ordered with everything in its proper place. This has clearly had a deep psychological impact as although they now know that cleaning and tidying are not naturally occurring phenomena, they carry on as if they were. I'm sure they wonder why I got rid of their self-making beds.

Keeping their clothes tidy and organised is a particular nightmare, at least for me. Let me paint a picture as Rog and Liv have developed their own approach.

Liv's room, above the waist, is pretty and serene. Pink (the actual colour is strangely named Fruitlands Quarter) with a crimson (Napier) feature wall. Teddy bears lounge in and dangle from a cargo net in the corner. But from waist down, it is a different story.

Liv prefers the floordrobe approach to clothes management. She sprinkles her clothes in a gentle, snow-like pattern lightly covering the carpet, bean bag, the end of her bed and any other flat surface. These clothes are not all destined for the washing basket, which stands empty an entire two metres from her door. No, many clothes will be reused. Her white – and that's a liberal use of the word – school socks are draped elegantly on her bean bag. She usually only brings one pair with her each week despite my constant nagging (yes, I can nag with the best of them) to bring all her clothes each week. These socks will be worn for five days. There's a pleasant thought for her schoolmates and teachers.

Near the enormous pile of stuffed toys, all those that couldn't fit in the cargo net, lie her favourite jeans. They are inside out with the underwear, Superman-like, still in place. She'll wear them again at the weekend, and the underwear, as nearly happened once, may fall out on her travels. That's a good look for a young lady.

Moving to Rog's room, it's eclectic which suits his personality. A large piano dominates one wall and shelves of models another. On the shelves are a range of toys and games unopened from previous birthdays and Christmas as well as a one-tenth completed replica of the *Titanic*. No problem with closure there.

Rog has mastered the clothing mountain. Do you remember the scene from *Close Encounters of the Third Kind* when Richard Dreyfuss builds his own replica of the Devil's Tower in his lounge? That's Rog's clothes. For those who haven't seen the movie, tip a full washing basket upside down. Perfect. Mixed together in his mound are clothes that are clean, dirty, some in between waiting to be re-worn and some that should be fumigated.

To my frustration, Rog enjoys the benefit of pockets. For him, and I suspect many boys, they are a cross between a rubbish bin and treasure trove. The amount of bric-a-brac I *find* is alarming enough, but it's the stuff that I miss that's the real problem. This I usually discover *after* I've done the washing – and a ruined load of washing is a particularly dispiriting experience. It sucks the joy out of life. Without delving into the reasons why, I've noticed that washing seems to be an exclusively feminine affair. I've certainly never heard a male exclaim at the start of a downpour, 'Shit, I've got the washing out.' Apart from myself that is.

When the children arrived for the week I used to lovingly put their clothes away for them. Then, on the following Sunday, I would empty all the drawers, add the washed clothes and put everything in neatly ordered piles so they could check and pack. Now they're old enough, beginning roughly from when Rog started high school, I have passed this responsibility to them. This now makes looking in their drawers a depressing experience and so I try not to. Mangled is the only way to describe their style of folding.

I used to police the putting away of clothes, but I lost faith after the following exchange with Rog:

'You're not putting them away like that are you?' I said in disbelief.

'What way?' Rog said, holding an arm full of clothes.

'You're missing the point of the exercise. Don't do it,' I said as I watched Rog move towards his chest of drawers.

'Do what?' He knew what.

'Don't. Do. It.'

'My McDonald's will get cold,' Rog replied as though that somehow made his intended action legitimate. I made a mental note to get *Supersize Me* out again. Then with a grin and the slightest shrug of his shoulders, Rog rammed his clothes into the drawer as if he was stuffing a cushion. I watched as he repeated the exercise until his suitcase was empty. There wasn't even any effort to keep like clothes together. Socks and shirts in the same drawer, how does that even work?

When he had finished, he stood up, smiling.

'If you look scruffy and unkempt, it's not my fault,' I said, shaking my head.

Rog again shrugged his shoulders.

'At least I'll know when you get your first girlfriend.' This time I'm smiling and Rog is wearing a confused look.

'You'll start being fussier with your clothes.'

The difficulty my children have changing the toilet roll sums up their ability to keep things ordered and tidy. To me, changing the toilet roll is a simple task and I've had this chat with them on multiple occasions. If the toilet roll is empty, you change it and put the empty roll in the recycling. That's all there is to it. In all my years as a single dad they haven't fully completed this task.

I have deciphered the logic they're using.

1. If they use the last of the roll, they leave the empty roll in place. They must feel lucky that there was just enough left for them. Hopefully.
2. If they find that the toilet roll is empty then they use the other toilet. They make it the next person's problem.

3. If this isn't possible as the other toilet is occupied or worse, and both toilet rolls are empty, then they take a new roll from the container I conveniently keep filled. But after use, they perch it on the empty roll or place it on top of the cistern.
4. If they feel like helping me out, they replace the toilet roll but leave the empty roll on top of the new roll or discard it under the bath for me to find and recycle it in a few months' time.

I'm generally relaxed about toilet etiquette, especially leaving the seat down, but flushing is mandatory and not optional. Speed or time of night is no excuse.

The children and I enjoy our chats about the toilet because we can't take it that seriously. And while the messages about cleanliness have been getting through of late, the toilet roll remains a mystery for them. I sense a conspiracy as they delight in the reaction the toilet roll brings. It is usually a couple of minutes of impromptu MacBeth.

Is this a toilet roll which I see before me? Come, let me replace thee.
I have thee not, and yet I see thee still. Chuck it hither, Banquo.

CHORES

In this environment I hope you're wondering how a single dad copes and stays sane. Maybe you're wondering how *you* cope and stay sane. Speaking for myself, I've put some measures in place that have allowed me to remain in the general population.

Through the course of this book you'll see that I'm quick to use financial incentives to reward the children for behaviour that I want to encourage. This comes straight from my management experience and let me assure you it works. There's a classic business article from the seventies by Stephen Kerr called 'On the folly of rewarding A, while hoping for B'. It's well worth a read, and unlike most academic articles it's very readable. The main point is that people, including children, do what's rewarded over what isn't rewarded.

For example, in business we pay directors a fee for attending meetings, rewarding A. But what we really want is engaged and dynamic directors, hoping for B. What do we get? Exactly what we pay for. High attendance – but do they add value? When you look at it in those terms it isn't rocket science.

With regard to my children, I was giving out pocket money for nothing but hoping they kept their rooms tidy and helped with chores. I was rewarding doing nothing and hoping for action. It was one of those 'Hang on, how dumb am I?' moments. So I started a system in which pocket money was linked to chores. I'm sure lots of parents do this.

To receive the maximum weekly payout, the children currently have to make breakfast and dinner once and have their room and computer area spotless at the end of the week. It's worked well. A warning, though – you have to be careful what you reward or you'll encourage behaviour you don't want. If I paid the children for changing the toilet roll, I'm sure the toilet roll would be changed alright – but multiple times a day. Children aren't mugs and I'd end up buying enough toilet paper for a family of nine.

To get action in other areas I had to do some lateral thinking. My children were using an incredible number of glasses on a daily basis. I found them in their rooms, on their desks, on the coffee table, on the mantelpiece and even near the dishwasher – though rarely *in* the dishwasher. To change this behaviour I bought them their very own glass, red for Rog and green for Liv. I have seen them rinsing and reusing those glasses. I ticked that off as a success, but it seems to have lapsed.

To keep on top of my domestic duties I treat them like the work they are and schedule them in my diary. I vacuum every Sunday, which is a simple task that makes a big difference to how the house looks. It's like mowing the grass, not that I mow the grass (see below for why). The toilets and bathrooms get cleaned once a month, which could be too much or too little but it seems to work. Dusting occurs when it's obvious or on the rare occasions when non-family visitors are expected.

The diary system works in the main but it's easy to ignore the reminders, often for weeks. For me it's usually a hangover that inspires a house-wide cleaning session. It's my way of trying to make the outside world look harmonious, countering what I feel like internally. I used to have cleaners come once a fortnight and they did a great job, but I needed them on post-children Monday when everyone else wanted them too. They came on Thursdays when I was solo and I found myself, like every other lunatic with cleaners, rushing around tidying the house before they came. I let them go, saved some money and made Thursdays less hectic at the same time.

Maintaining the section and garden became easy after I did the math. I totalled the cost of a lawn-mower, petrol and maintenance, weed eater and the various gardening tools and sprays required. Then I added in my time and lack of gardening knowledge and the decision to hire a lawn-mowing service and a gardener becomes obvious. They save me time and money, and the outside of my house has never looked better. It's good for local businesses too.

DOMESTIC DETAILS

With plans in place, covering off the well-known domestic tasks in a timely fashion is fairly straightforward. It's the subtler areas I struggle with. I'm aware I risk eyeball rolling from more domestically able readers so I apologise in advance, but there are domesticity aspects which remain a mystery to me, despite the length of time I've been single. For example, when is it time to change the sheets? And why do people make such a big fuss about clean sheets? A female friend has a weekly 'clean sheet' day when everyone looks forward to the apparent joy of snuggling into them. Weekly feels at one end of the domestic diligence continuum – but should they be changed bi-weekly, or monthly? Obviously you should change them if you hope to have company and that can make it somewhat variable. If you're an optimist, like me, then hope means they get changed more frequently than required. Probably a good thing.

It's the same problem for all the towels and mats dotted around the house. Tea towels and bath mats start to look manky, which is a convenient clue, but the rest of mine usually look pretty clean (a benefit of buying dark colours). I change them haphazardly, such as when I'm hungover, or when it feels that the items in questions are pushing the boundaries of decency.

Washing clothes is a task I save for the weekend. In other words, I refuse to do it until the weekend. Rose used to keep me away from the washing machine, obviously valuing her clothes, but over the years I've progressed to at least competent. I separate the washing into piles of whites and colours and wash them with the same programme: slightly soiled whites and delicate colours. It seems to work. I'm smart enough, meaning I have paid the odd high-priced lesson, not to use this method on more expensive items such as suits and jackets. They go, on rare occasions, to the drycleaners.

I have not time for, and deliberately ignore, the stupid washing instructions attached to many clothing items. Does anyone read those until the item is out of shape, faded or both? For a start, the writing is miniscule and, in the dim light of the laundry, it may as well be written in invisible ink. If I had a scanning electron microscope handy, they make each item sound like they're from Louis Vuitton or Gucci. By way of example, there were six instructions that I was meant to observe on Liv's low-cost sweatshirt:

- WASH WITH SIMILAR COLOURS. Okay, it took a few disasters but I now observe the whites versus colours law.
- GENTLE MACHINE WASH WARM. Nice grammar. Everything is washed in cold water because that's what's written on the packet of washing powder.
- DO NOT SOAK OR BLEACH. Liv's jacket is no danger of proactive attention.

- RESHAPE WHILE DAMP. Into what? It entered in the shape of a jacket and I expect it to come out the shape of a jacket.
- COOL TUMBLE DRY ON LOW. I use the dryer only for socks and underwear because I don't have enough clothes pegs, line space and patience.
- COOL IRON ON REVERSE IF NEEDED. Needed? Ironing is not needed, wanted or desired. Hung or folded are the only two actions that happen to washed clothes. I iron business shirts on an as-required basis.

Washing instructions are as useful as the warning 'Not dishwasher safe'. They shouldn't be allowed to sell kitchen items with that warning. They may as well write 'Use only once'. I know all the items in my kitchen are dishwasher safe because that's been sorted out by my Darwinian dishwasher. Survival of the fittest.

Less-frequent chores include cleaning the oven, which is a joyless task that can be avoided for years. If the light in the oven worked, which it doesn't, it wouldn't be any use and that alone tells me it's due for a clean. The oven probably needs replacing and not solely to avoid cleaning it. The front gas element takes an age to light and then goes out at least twice before doing its job, causing bad language to emanate from the chef. The oven door doesn't close properly either, although I have rigged a bungee cord that I wrap around the handle to keep it in place when cooking. It's not an aesthetically pleasing solution, but it stops heat from escaping.

The dishwasher needs replacing as well. The door catch has broken and the only way to get the dishwasher to recognise the door is closed and start is to jam it closed with a bamboo stake, borrowed from the tomatoes, that's wedged into the floor. This works but doesn't always stop water from leaking. An additional local hazard is that because the catch is broken, the door delights in crashing down of its own accord which is loud and extremely unsettling. This again causes the chef's language to change. Especially when I slow the door's speed with my leg.

The children are, I hope, impressed with my kitchen ingenuity, but that's because they don't have to use the oven or dishwasher on a regular basis. I can't imagine a significant other would be either impressed or content. Rose wouldn't have put up with it for very long.

All in all it's a mental effort rather than a physical one that's required to keep on top of the domestic duties. I hope I haven't given you the impression that my house is in a state. It isn't. The kitchen, with its unique solutions, looks normal because the bungees and bamboo are hidden from view until required. And unless you're actually using the towels or sheets, everything appears ordered and presentable. When I'm alone the mess I make is limited to a tiny footprint and when the children are with me I'm fastidious as I want them to be in a home that looks and feels clean. My logic is that if the house is kept clean, they will be encouraged to keep it clean as well. One day anyway.

Reflections

- *Children create mess. It's a natural phenomenon.*
- *Don't expect your children to notice your domestic accomplishments. They won't thank you for doing the laundry, they simply want to know where you have put their underwear. It's okay.*
- *Changing a toilet roll is too complex for anyone under the age of eighteen to understand. That's okay too.*
- *Using money to focus your children's attention on what chores you want them to do works brilliantly. Care is required to ensure what you reward is the behaviour you want to encourage.*
- *Change your sheets and towels when they need to be changed. That's as much as I know about that.*
- *Scheduling domestic tasks in your diary is a handy way to make sure you don't forget them. You can still ignore them.*
- *Washing instructions on clothes are designed to stop you demanding your money back when the washing goes bad!*

10. The Bachelor Week

Bachelors should be heavily taxed. It is not fair that some men should be happier than others.
Oscar Wilde (playwright, novelist and poet, 1854–1900)

You may think that when I don't have the children I spend my time in a frenzy of bachelor-related activity. Every second week as free as a bird. I can chase fast women and slow horses, drink as much as I like and abandon any thoughts of fashion decency, at least at home. I can watch TV with no negotiation: endless sport, no bloody cooking shows, soaps or worse, reality TV.

I admit that bachelor weeks do probably sound like fun. When I was married, and Rog and Liv were babies, the concept of coming home to a quiet house, grabbing a beer and watching the *News* with my feet on the table felt similar in my mind to an overseas holiday. Work trips were fantastic for that reason, they gave me legitimate time out. 'Of course I'd rather be home with you and the little darlings, hun, but I have to spend five days (and nights) in a hotel in Brisbane at a damned all-expenses-paid conference.'

Karma is never far away, though.

I was away for a night in Auckland when Rog was three and Liv one. I was looking forward to the trip with carefully concealed delight. That night, as I slept peacefully without the risk of young lungs demanding attention, I was violently woken around 3am by what sounded like a brick hitting the motel window. Violent noise in the wee small hours is never good news. I lay quiet and tense listening for further activity, contemplating what action to take. My fight-or-flight response was pounding blood in my ears but there was now a deathly silence. I slowly unstiffened and put the episode down to drunken hooligans walking through the carpark. Hoping they suffered a nasty fate, I went back to sleep.

An hour later, boom, another brick-like attack occurred. I couldn't believe it. Had I taken the wrong flight and landed in Syria? This time I was up. Every muscle was twitching. I stormed out the door to confront the perpetrators. I hadn't entirely thought through what I was going to do against a pack of drunken hooligans, but I was saved from the dilemma because the car park was deserted. No hooligans, no bricks, no damage, no nothing. WTF? I retreated back inside mystified – and wide, wide awake. This time I struggled to fall asleep waiting for the next whatever, which never came. I woke in my usual sleep-deprived and dishevelled state.

It was when I got the milk out of the fridge for breakfast that I discovered the cause of last night's 'attacks'. The fridge thermostat had broken, the motel owner confirmed this, turning the fridge into a freezer. As the temperature plummeted, two coke cans had exploded with such force they looked like the shredded remains of two explosive devices. The fridge, naturally in a motel room, was right next to the bed. Right next to my ear in fact. That's karma in all its glory.

I'm sure the odd week of freedom would be heaven for most parents. It would be like a holiday, but it loses its gloss when it's the norm. Hotels are a great escape, a luxury, but on your own they quickly become mind-numbingly boring. The rooms are the size of a shoe box with a tiny bathroom, and after a few long hours I often feel the overwhelming desire to escape. Weeks by yourself have a tendency to feel similar.

So let me wander you through one of my typical bachelor weeks. You can see if the grass is as green as you suspect, or hope for. First, a reminder: although I was alone I was in a relationship, so the pursuit of fast women wasn't an option. Besides, wandering around bars in my forties is rather a depressing thought.

Freedom starts after I drop the children off on Sunday at 6pm. Much of Sunday has been spent carrying out the exciting tasks of washing, folding clothes, tidying, organising and matching impossibly similar socks. Sorting the children's clothes has got harder as they've grown and their clothes now look similar to each other's and mine. I make sure everything's in order for the handover as Monday morning and school are only a few hours away. At the handover Rose and I compare notes on the past week and what's on in the coming week: events, sports, visits to the orthodontist for Liv, etc. I get big hugs, from Rog and Liv that is, and I'm gone. Free.

I buy supplies on the way home to replenish the fridge and cupboards that the children have cleaned out locust-like. It doesn't take long as I only need enough for one. I then arrive home to a stillness that has supplanted the lively atmosphere of an hour ago. I usually spend Sunday evening catching up on work, writing, watching TV and trying not to drink – at least too much. Alcohol relaxes and provides an escape but it gets the week off on the wrong foot.

When I feel tired, which after a week with the children isn't that late, I slope off to bed and read whatever novel I have on the go. I like authors such as Michael Connolly and Lee Child, as you can get through their books quickly. In a moment of classical inspiration I once started, but never finished, Dostoyevsky's *Crime and Punishment*. That was hard work for bedtime reading.

WEEK DAYS

Monday through Friday mornings are much of a muchness. I plan to start my days early so my alarm – Reggie singing 'Better', is set for 5am. This is an aspirational alarm which is immediately silenced.

The reality alarm goes off at 6.30am though I hit the snooze button a various number of times before reluctantly abandoning bed and turning on the jug for coffee. Cathy witnessed this on a visit and seemed appalled. I was confused because the jug was the focus of her disapproval.

I discovered Cathy insists that the jug is filled freshly each morning as, in her words, 'who knows what's crawled in during the night?' I'm less fussy – way less fussy – and that extended to boiling the jug when I returned from a three-week trip to the UK. It took a few cups of coffee to work out that the strange flavour of formic acid was coming from the boiled ants in the jug and not, as I had concluded, the hidden ants in the coffee jar. Just why I suspected the coffee jar, an airtight container, and not the jug on the bench I put down to jetlag. Unfortunately, I discovered the truth after I'd disposed of the coffee on suspicion. The bonus of Cathy's fear – let's not call it paranoia – was that she made the coffee in the morning. There were no complaints from me.

I switch on a news channel and think about breakfast but usually settle for more coffee. I check emails and the internet to see what's gone on in the world overnight and check what the upcoming day looks like. The most critical question I have to answer is – do I need to wear a suit? Image and brand are important in business and I wear a suit in business situations, but if my diary is clear of client appointments I dress casually. Once I've developed a plan of attack for the day, I quickly shower and head off with high hopes of productivity.

I start in my office at the university, which is my base for work and study. I check emails and appointments again to make sure I'm on top of the day then delay starting by getting more coffee. I realise that my coffee intake is quite high and I try and avoid it past lunchtime. This was after a chat with a GP cricket friend who said that it could disturb sleep if taken later in the day. I haven't noticed that coffee impacts on me often apart from the odd time when after a particularly strong brew I feel wired.

Once I'm ready to start I attack the tasks that demand my brain be at its sharpest. This is usually study and is accompanied by classical music, which helps drown out distractions as well as creating an old-world, library-like ambiance.

If I don't have many appointments, lunch becomes the highlight of the day. For about two years three student colleagues and I had bonded into an international lunch club. We had representatives from Indonesia (Uri), China (Lei), Malaysia (Lyn) and New Zealand (me) and we spent an enjoyable hour chatting. I told Kiwi jokes that they didn't understand but listened politely to, while they found New Zealand colloquialisms and the pronunciation of words like 'bald' hilarious. We were an eclectic group.

Occasionally I had fun at their expense. It was never nasty, I just took advantage of the language differences that appealed to my sometimes infantile sense of humour. One memorable one ran as follows.

'What do you do for fun in Malaysia, Lyn?' It was an innocent question intended to spark up the conversation.

'We go ten-pin bowling. It's big back home.'

'How often?'

'There's a league at my uni, so most weeks. I have balls!'

I looked around. My colleagues' faces were dead serious. Clearly they thought that Lyn having balls wasn't remotely funny. I suppressed anything but a slight smile and carried the conversation on.

'How many balls have you got?'

'I have two balls.'

'I was hoping you did.'

'Pardon?'

'Nothing, carry on.' The rest of the table remained silent and sober.

'I have a thirteen kg ball and an eleven I use for spares,' Lyn informed me without a flicker.

'Impressive. Have you played much in New Zealand?'

'Some. I went with some friends and my supervisor, Deek.'

'Deek?'

'Deek.'

'Richard?'

'Yesssss.' Lyn had a lovely way of drawing out words she emphasised.

'Ahhh ... It's pronounced Dick.' Balls and dick, this was eighties British comedy at its finest.

'Deek.' Lyn tried saying it slowly but there was no discernible change.

'Close enough. Does Dick have his own balls?'

'Deek had no balls.'

I politely excused myself at that point, leaving behind confused looks from my charming colleagues. They would have heard me laughing all the way back to my office. I'm sure they'll forgive me, especially Lyn.

Two to three times a week after work I head to an instructor-led gym or karate class. The gym is attached to the university and the majority of people who attend the popular classes are young female students. I'm not sure why the classes aren't attractive to males. A typical class consists of mainly eighteen to twenty-five-year-old females with a few males of a similar age and a thin sprinkling of male and female 'mature athletes', like me.

The only time the gender ratio has been remotely close to fifty/fifty was when there were only two of us. I thought the trainer would cancel, in fact I hoped she would, but we did the entire fifty-five-minute class as per normal, which was surreal. There was no chance of taking the usual breather by blending into the crowd during that class.

Apart from the fitness aspect, the other reason I like the gym and karate is that they extend the time until I head home to my lovely but quiet house. I even look forward to the gym on a Friday night when most people are keen to get home early or head somewhere for a drink. Nigel Marsh in his entertaining book *Fat, Forty and Fired* wrote about sitting in his car dreading going into the house at what he called 'arsenic hour'. The time when the chaos of dinner, baths, homework and bedtime are all in full flight. Well, even given that Nigel had four children, after experiencing the polar opposite for years I'd take the chaos.

Emptiness carries a weight that the TV's chattering does little to lighten. I understand why people rush inadvisably into new relationships to try and recapture a 'normal' life. But without all the other necessary ingredients for a successful relationship, they're simply jumping from the frying pan into the fire.

When I finally return home some form of dinner is needed. As described, cooking and eating solo aren't fun, but I need to eat and I'm usually starving so I'll cobble together something that resembles dinner or devour the kebab purchased on the way home. Eating takes much less time than cooking, so after I pile the dishes on the bench I'm done. Cleaning the kitchen can wait for the morning. Or the next morning.

I'm now free to hit the town, but at 8pm I never feel up to a bachelor-like ran-tan. If I can lever myself off the couch I can usually be found working, studying or writing. I sometimes contemplate going to the movies and for a short while I got into the habit of doing so once a week. If going to the movies by yourself sounds sad, it isn't that bad. The aspect I missed the most was chatting afterwards. Everyone sees a slightly different movie and it's interesting to hear what other people think. Now my children are older I'm able to have wonderful conversations with them after movies like *The Life of Pi* and what they thought about the tiger.

THE WEEKEND

That's the week taken care of, almost. Friday night is now looming large. Woo-hoo. First a small confession. I'm not as devoted to exercise as I may have led you to believe and I've been known to miss the gym on Friday night in favour of a drink with friends and colleagues. The local pub is a popular spot and it soon becomes crowded, noisy and somewhat intimate. Getting to and from the bar requires nimble footwork in order to avoid rubbing up against too many people.

I've noticed that our band of getting-merry men resembles the crowd at a tennis match. Heads turning left and right as women wander to and from the bar. It's not an exclusive male group trait and I've seen female groups watching the same rally. I'm not sure whether I find it funny or depressing when I catch my own head tracking left or right.

While it's fun to catch up with colleagues over a drink, I try not to stay too long and leave well before the evening gets into full swing. The crowd changes, the music gets louder and ties and morals are loosened or abandoned.

I start weekends slowly. Sleeping in usually isn't an option as I'm a regular at the children's sport whether I'm off duty or not. The children love me watching and I love to watch them charge about. I arrive with my obligatory coffee and, if the circumstances dictate, something greasy like a giant sausage roll for breakfast.

I'm pleased to report that while watching my children play, I'm a model parent. I don't care who wins or loses as long as *everyone* has fun. Really! I do *prefer* if our team wins, but you'll never see me strutting up and down the sideline yelling obscenities at the referee.

Saturday afternoon is blocked out for work or study, but unless there is a deadline imminent it's hard to find the required motivation. Depending on the weather, I may potter around the garden, catch up on some reading or watch sport on TV. In the summer there's cricket to follow and in the winter I love the NRL (Australian rugby league).

That brings us to Saturday evening, which for many people is the social highlight of the week. A time for parties and gatherings. For me it's a much quieter affair, partly by choice, partly by circumstance, and I usually spend Saturday night alone. It's okay, but it leans towards dull and the option to kick back with a beer at 5pm is attractive. I had thought that having a drink related to the nautical time when the sun is over the yard arm. Research via *QI* informed me the sun is over the yard arm around 11am and was when sailors had their first tot of rum. Interesting but I'm sticking to 5pm all the same.

As Saturday evening wears on, attention gets drawn once more towards food, but by Saturday the fridge and cupboards are suffering from Old Mother Hubbard syndrome. I've hopefully bought something on the way home from sport or wandered into the supermarket but, if not, it's a good opportunity to eat all those items that otherwise would be binned. Questionable dips, dodgy packets of cold meat, limp vegetables and assorted leftovers from the week. That's a meal you won't see on anyone's menu planner.

I have a tendency to fall asleep on my comfortable couch on Saturday night. Late in the evening, or early in the morning, I wake to a different game. Usually a different sport. The Cronulla Sharks playing the Melbourne Storm has become HNK Rijeka playing GNK Dinamo Zagreb. It's disorientating for a few moments until I track down the remote and silence the unintelligible over-excited European commentator and struggle off to bed. When the children are with me I'm extra vigilant with security but when it's only me, I'm lax. I have awoken to discover doors and windows unlocked or open. Cathy is once again appalled and surprised I haven't been murdered in my bed.

Finally it's Sunday. I used to play golf religiously, which required an early start, but I haven't swung a club in years after work and study got hectic. I make coffee, tidy the kitchen and watch the end of the sport I missed but hopefully recorded. At midday I head to my mum's for Sunday lunch, a tradition since I can remember, before visiting the supermarket to once again stock up the cupboards and fridge for the imminent arrival of my hungry children.

Just before 6pm it's time to dive back into domestic duties and kick the house into shape. I do the vacuuming, make sure the bathrooms are clean and, of course, replenish the toilet rolls. Before you know it, Rog and Liv are back, scattering their possessions and dispelling the silence for another week. They always look taller …

That, my friends, is the exciting, fashionable and glamorous lifestyle of a not so rich and famous single dad on his bachelor week. Keen to trade? One simple way to avoid joining me is to get home earlier on Friday night with your tie still knotted.

Reflections

- Weeks by yourself as a single dad are often the hardest, but you get used to them. Filling the void with just anyone is a bad idea on many levels.
- If you are hanging out in a bar and can't spot the oldest person within two minutes, it's you. Go home.
- It's okay to relax your domestic standards when no one is around, only don't let them slide too far. There's always the chance of a surprise visitor.
- Try to limit alcohol, and other avenues, as a means of escape. It's an easy trap to fall into when the house is quiet.
- Exercise is a positive way to spend some of that time that's in abundance. A hobby you love would also work. Try to find something productive.
- Empty and refill the jug when you have been away on holiday. Surprise flavours aren't welcome.

11. A Tale of Two Houses

It was the best of times, it was the worst of times.
Charles Dickens (writer, 1812-70)

Fifty-fifty shared care is excellent in principle and a lot of research supports the view that children are best served when both parents are a major factor in their lives. Each parent takes full responsibility for raising the children but they split the time so the children get equal time with mum and dad. In my experience to make this work smoothly requires logistics and communication.

My business experience has taught me that logistics aren't easy. Plans are easy to develop conceptually – the difficulties may emerge only during implementation. The saying 'No plan survives contact with the enemy', attributed to Helmuth von Moltke the Elder, is very apt.

An example from my early IT days highlighted this to me. Our company wanted to save money on a mailout to clients and decided to do it ourselves. It sounded simple. Print out the ten-page document for each client plus their policies, pop them all in a windowed envelope, post them and Bob's your uncle. I was brought in to help make it happen. However, when I crunched the numbers I discovered that it would need our fastest printer to run non-stop for three weeks, be replenished with toner every few hours and with paper almost constantly. I passed on my initial concerns with some additional questions. Can we buy paper by the pallet? How will we get it to the seventh floor? Is the floor strong enough?

The job was outsourced. Many colleagues have heard me say this, but the devil is *always* in the detail.

Two homes meant the children had two bedrooms. Rose and I weren't keen to duplicate the bedroom contents and therefore our logistics problem was how to transport the content of their rooms from house to house each Sunday. Clothes, books, toys, games, mementos, posters, school bags, piano, sports gear, game consoles, etc. Can you picture what that looks like? I can, because that's more or less how we started in the early days. Except for the piano. Even today we resemble refugees escaping an oncoming army, fire, flood or pestilence taking our worldly possessions with us. I gave up trying to pare things down.

'Liv, you don't have to take so many teddies, you have dozens at your mum's.'

'I *need* them all.'

'What about leaving Yeti behind? He's huge.'

During 2009 we became hooked on watching the Tour de France over breakfast. Liv fell in love with the toy yetis they handed out to the leader of the young rider classification and Cathy set out to get her one for a birthday present. The problem was that the Le Tour yeti was cute and the size of a loaf of bread. The one they sold was five times the size. Not deterred, Cathy bought one and then employed a range of origami techniques and folded him/her into a small cardboard box and posted him/her via the Royal Mail. Where the Customs form requires a description of the goods, she had written 'he/she is a yeti'. Given this description the parcel had been inspected by Customs and there was a small cut in the packaging where I assume they tested his/her fur to make sure he/she wasn't real. That must have made a strange scene, checking to see if a mythical creature's fur was real ...

'He has to come, he's family.' Liv's tone indicates the outrageous argument has concluded.

'Fine,' I say and wince immediately. I hate that particular four-letter F word. 'Fine' is the word some people, more commonly considered to be members of the fairer sex, use to end an argument when they consider they're right but can't stand to hear your voice any longer. In my experience it's usually said with closed eyes because they can't stand to look at you either.

I turn to Rog, hoping to be able to set an example for Liv.

'You don't want to take big bear, do you?'

'What?'

He doesn't have to say anything else. His look of incomprehension says it all. I'm beaten. Besides, does it really matter? As long as I can get everything in the car and make one trip it's ... *fine*. In hindsight, I suspect being able to take everything helped the children feel more in control of the two-house arrangement.

Over the years Rose and I have tweaked our approach and whittled down the amount transported to a more manageable level. Aiding this has been Rog and Liv getting tired of the time it takes them to pack. We still transport a carload but, as they have grown, they've also acquired more stuff, especially clothes. Latterly I've made them responsible for their own packing but it pays to keep a wary parental eye on the process – if they forget things, it's Rose and I that do the running around.

COMMUNICATION AND COUNSELLING

If you're able to sort out the logistics there's the tricky area of communication to overcome. Couples who've separated on the nicest terms must still struggle with communication, at least initially. After our separation the contact between Rose and I was the sort you have with Inland Revenue. It's civil, reserved and with little enjoyment or enthusiasm.

We were miles away from where we are today, but when I compared notes with other separated friends, we weren't that bad. Bitterness, revenge and lawyers seem to be the common themes. Rose and my post-separation communication seemed at the friendlier end of the scale.

There were a couple of issues where Rose and I differed. Even with our better-than-average communication, there appeared little chance of navigating our way through them by ourselves. Rose suggested we try family counselling.

The Kiwi bloke's – i.e. *my* – attitude to counselling is that except in serious circumstances it's not necessary. It's a bit new-age, tree-hugging and hippyish. I'm fully aware that this attitude is dated and unhelpful but I'm a product of my environment (though I am trying to evolve). At the time counselling struck me as unnecessary and I thought we should sort out the issues ourselves. Rose made it clear she was keen to try counselling, and in the interests of world peace, or at least the piece of the world I was in, I agreed.

A friend of Rose's had recommended a counsellor and we arrived punctually for our first session. We'd been separated for around a month and in the car park I noticed that she'd bought herself a new car. I have no idea about the makes and models of cars but it was hard to miss that the dark-blue SUV was now a sleek-looking, fire-engine-red Mazda.

'Nice car,' I said to make conversation. 'I thought you'd have bought a people mover, hun.'

'You would, wouldn't you,' came the extremely icy reply. 'And don't call me *hun*.'

I flinched internally at my slip. I found it difficult to stop calling her 'hun'. I'd been doing it for sixteen years. All the same, I didn't feel the use of the word warranted such a cool reaction. Before we separated Rose had been trying to convince me that we should buy a people mover but I hated them. They look like loaves of bread on wheels. Perfect for taxis but very uncool, and not desirable for small, fashionable families like ours. With my opinion no longer a factor I thought that she'd buy one.

It was later that evening, as I recounted this exchange to Cathy, that I was reminded of the email I'd forwarded to Rose which had inadvertently contained part of a conversation I was having in which I had a rant against people movers. This explained the icy reply. Although I was just trying to be friendly, I'd managed to piss Rose off twice in a twelve-word sentence. It wasn't an auspicious start to counselling but thankfully I was, at that stage, blissfully unaware of the second part of my faux pas.

We were ushered into the counsellor's room and we sat on separate couches in a tense silence. The room looked like a cross between a rumpus room and a doctor's waiting room. There were toys spread around the room and *Woman's Weekly*-type magazines on a small table that was the focus of the room. There was no desk or computer; this room was clearly for counselling only. The counsellor's credentials were proudly displayed on the walls.

Pat was a qualified marriage guidance counsellor, family counsellor (which explained the room's layout) and sex therapist (which didn't explain the room's layout). It was an interesting mix of qualifications but they were all related in a fashion. Then a sudden thought hit me. Pat? I was assuming Pat was a she. The name Pat could easily be a he. Patrick, a jovial Irishman with a massive red beard. I couldn't imagine a sex therapist with a beard.

She, or he, was taking their time, leaving Rose and I in an awkward quiet. My mind started to wander to how sex therapy sessions were conducted but thankfully that train of thought was interrupted by the arrival of Pat, who was to my relief a she. She looked exactly like what I imagined a counsellor and sex therapist should look like. I'll leave the rest to your imagination.

After the introductions, Pat told us that this session was focused on establishing the ground rules for the counselling and to identify what we were trying to achieve. We were then given the opportunity to express our thoughts and feelings. Rose went first and, I must confess, I wasn't listening as I was busy trying to work out what I was going to say. When it was my turn I gave what I considered was an appropriate response as, sitting with a counsellor and sex therapist and my ex, nobody needed to hear what was in my head. It was lost on me at the time that that's the entire point of counselling. Clearly some evolving was, and probably is, still needed.

The focus then turned to the issues we were having – our difficulty in finding a middle ground for our parenting differences. We each expressed our opinion on these issues and what we thought was required for resolution. The specifics aren't important, but suffice to say that we each thought the other should change, which wasn't a major surprise.

The session didn't last long, about twenty minutes. Time flies when you're having fun. We agreed to keep the conversation flowing if possible and to meet in a week's time. We also agreed to keep a joint notebook which was to be held by the parent who had the children. If we noticed anything that we thought the other parent should know we were to jot it down. The notes were only to refer to matters concerning the children. So 'Rog has been looking worried' is fine but 'You've put on weight you fat git' wasn't (that was just the example we used). The notebook was to be passed over at the Sunday handover. I thought that this was a sensible idea.

Back in the car park I watched Rose drive away, sunglasses on in her new snazzy red car. I was left with mixed feelings regarding counselling. I felt we could have achieved as much via email but, on the whole, it seemed useful and certainly harmless. It was going to let us discuss our issues in an open and civilised manner. The alternative path promised protracted debate and stalemate. I didn't dwell on it because I was still intrigued why she hadn't bought a people mover.

The next counselling session was, in my view, more productive. We descended quickly into the nitty-gritty and the areas of difference between us were openly debated. The counsellor, while remaining neutral, seemed to agree with my stance and hinted that Rose may need to make some modifications. Rose became … quiet. We bounced around the topic, as you do during counselling, and Rose agreed to take on board the feedback. I thought that this counselling lark wasn't so bad after all. We were clearly making progress.

That was our last counselling session. Rose informed me via email that I was right, counselling was a complete waste of time. The irony. Not that it mattered greatly as slowly, very slowly as I recollect, the issues resolved themselves. We kept the diary system running for a few months, and it proved valuable until things settled down.

I'm not sure 'until things settled down' is an accurate reflection of that time. When you reflect from your comfortable position in the present it's difficult to transport yourself back in time, especially at an emotional level. Memorable facts, events, dates and times are relatively easy to remember, like the time I found Liv crying in the cupboard. But the uneventful days and weeks merge into one amorphous blob and more recent memory gradually over-writes the images and feelings.

When I take myself back to those early handovers, when the children must have been confused and unsettled, I see and feel today's handovers. Happy, well-adjusted children with Rose and I having a cup of tea and chatting like old friends. It was nothing like that. It wasn't nasty, but it was tense and it wasn't fun. The exchanges were quick and functional and were conducted at the front door. Drop the children and gear off, exchange news in clipped sentences and away again. They took no more than a minute, leaving only mutual sighs of relief.

It takes a lot of mental effort to recapture Rog and Liv as they were in those early exchanges. They were quiet and they watched our exchanges closely while looking uninterested. I would sweep them up and we would get stuck into something, anything. Distraction worked for me as well as I hope it did for them.

That's why, with the sharp edges of memory blunted by time, I'd love to write that it didn't take long until the handovers became normal. Is six months long? Was it six months? What's normal? When we stopped using the diary the handovers were becoming ordinary and I honestly believe that the children have adapted well to the week-on/week-off routine. Rose and I put in a lot of effort emotionally to make it work and it became simply the way it was. Day by day, week by week, month by month it continued to improve until …

FLYING SOLO

'Head Office has moved to Wellington and I have to move as well. It's only two hours away and so we need to alter things,' Rose repeated calmly.

'WHAT?' I said, far less calmly.

Rose having to shift with her company derailed our period of glasnost and plunged us back to the cold war. It had been nearly two years since we separated and over that time there'd been a lot of bridge building. Things were running smoothly, at least that's what I thought, and the past was being slowly buried. Rose's move lobbed a grenade under the bridge.

I'd taken the significant step of starting a PhD programme while still running my consulting business. The decision was based on our week-on/week-off arrangement, as every other week I had time and space to schedule lots of work, study and out-of-town travel.

Rose and I discussed possible options, mainly via email. Rose was keen to explore the idea of everyone moving to Wellington. I wasn't. It would mean that the children and I would be starting anew. With this option sidelined, we were left with one viable way forward. The children would live with me in the week and Rose would pick them up Friday evening, have them for the weekend and drop them back on Sunday evening. As I loved watching the children's sporting exploits on Saturdays, this meant that I would become a full-time dad with time off for good, or bad, behaviour on Friday and Saturday nights.

I was torn. As much as I loved the idea of more time as a trio, I realised that my plans for work and study would suffer. I decided that if it had to be this way – and it appeared a fait accompli – then changes were needed so not only would I cope, I'd enjoy the change. The last thing the children needed was a grumpy dad around *all* the time.

First, my nanny, Sam, as a poor student, was more than happy to double her income and nanny on both weeks allowing me to retain full work days. My mum was available, including the odd overnight, if required. This proved to be invaluable when Rog or Liv were sick or I had to travel. Bit by bit the logistics fell into place and I started to believe that this might turn out exciting. At least I think that's what I thought – or maybe that last sentence is another example of the present colouring the past. If I'm honest, I was probably still quite dark about everything.

Cathy also had concerns about the new arrangements. In particular she was anxious that I make sure Rose kept to the agreed times and arrived each Friday at 6pm as agreed. Much of Cathy's concern came from her own hard-earned lessons. For her, pick-up times were often unilaterally pushed back or sometimes completely missed to suit last-minute changes in her ex's social calendar. It meant she was unable to plan with any certainty. She was concerned that what happened to her would happen to me.

She was right to be concerned. The scheduled Friday pick-up was regularly delayed due to meetings, traffic or both. The new arrangements meant I was, in theory, off-duty at 6pm, but Sam finished at six and I was having to cover this gap. I confess that this usually meant leaving the pub earlier than planned, but it was the principle involved that concerned me. I shouldn't have to leave the pub early or miss a gym class.

I gave Rose some 'feedback' and the situation was remedied by Rose organising her mum to pick up the children. While this worked for the adults involved, I noticed Rog and Liv both frowned when I explained the new situation. I guess they were looking forward to seeing their mum and in hindsight it may have been another case of getting the logistics right but missing the point.

I must balance this episode as it wasn't all one-way traffic. Some weeks Rose would leave early, so the children were delighted when they found Mum waiting for them after school. This did, however, usually happen only at the last minute and so Sam was delighted as well. She got a free paid afternoon as I felt I needed to give her more than a few hours' warning that she wasn't needed.

TIGER

The new childcare arrangements saw the number of occupants in my home increase by one making us a four, although it was not the definitive nuclear family. Two weeks before we were due to start the new arrangements Rose and I had an email exchange over the final details, which I have massaged into a conversation so you get the gist.

'So that's everything settled,' I said. 'We start in a fortnight.'

'Yep,' replied Rose. 'I'll drop the gear off on Sunday. You'll have to organise for the piano to be shifted.'

'The piano?'

'It makes no sense leaving it my place. If it's at your house Rog can practise.'

'Good thinking.' I thought the conversation was over until Rose said, almost as an afterthought, 'And you need to take your cats.'

'*My* cats?'

Our separation agreement had made no mention of our two remaining cats, Tiger and Gnu. At one point we had five, mainly thanks to the litter our cat Tangles produced unexpectedly. My well-aimed shoe hadn't been as effective as I'd thought in breaking up Tangles' liaison with Eddie, the neighbour's cat. As Rose kept the house and that's where the cats were, she naturally kept them too. This had been fine right up until now.

There's a mandatory clause in all New Zealand separation agreements that roughly states that at the time the separation becomes official, all remaining property not specifically identified in the settlement is owned by whoever has possession. This makes sense as a clear split is achieved so arguments over who owns what can't linger. Rose and I agreed we would share a range of items communally, such as the camping gear, but this had to be a 'gentleman's agreement' – it couldn't be legally recognised.

Even though two years had passed, with Rose working out of town the cats had in her eyes reverted to being *my* cats. I may be doing Rose a discredit here (though I'm not sure), but she may have been subtly working on me for some time. She had mentioned, unsolicited, how sad Tiger had been lately and that he was missing me. And how the children talked about not having a cat at my house.

Rose and I debated the cat situation via email and, as much as I love cats, I was reluctant. When I travelled for work, study or on holiday I'd have the same problem Rose was now facing. In effect, she was making her problem my problem. In the end I agreed to take one, Tiger. My logic was that given his age, fifteen, which is good for a cat, and love of company I thought he may not survive without people around. Gnu, on the other hand, was younger and settled at Rose's. The twist in this story was that ultimately Rose organised to have family members move into her house. After all the debate Tiger could have stayed put, but he settled in immediately at my place and it seemed to me he'd just been waiting for an invitation.

It was lovely having Tiger around. He was one of Tangles' litter and so had been with us since he was zero. He was an affectionate old thing too and I would find him waiting patiently in the driveway when I came home. That part was lovely, but he normally wouldn't budge despite my leaning on the horn. I would get out of the car and pick him up. He would then nervously travel the last twenty metres up the drive on my lap. The children loved having him around too and even Cathy, who insisted she didn't like pets, would open the door each morning during her visits excitedly calling 'Poofy, Poofy, Poofy'.

The only downside was Tiger's age, seventy-seven in human years, which created the odd cleaning issue that demanded immediate attention.

BACK TO THE FUTURE

Even allowing for my blunted memory, it didn't take long for Rog, Liv, Tiger and I to get used to the new world order. In many respects I found it much easier. I was now solely responsible for day-to-day life and so I knew everything that was going on at school and everything that needed to happen after school. The children's things were at my house, meaning the often laborious Sunday swapping of clothes and equipment was a thing of the past. There was also less debate about what sports and activities they would attend. I got to call the shots, in consultation with Rose and the children of course. Everything was under control. That's probably a massive over-statement, but that's how it felt.

My home became home and we became an extremely tight unit. Of course there was no 'Mum' figure during the week, though I found that this had an unexpected plus. It meant that the children and I became even closer as I had to work on developing my feminine side, which I don't think is a bad thing. Especially as I achieved this without developing moobs.

Being a near solo dad certainly changed the relationship trajectory for the children and me. It's easy to take for granted our closeness but it doesn't take much reflection to know how different the world could have been. Would Liv snuggle into me on the couch as much as she does? Or would Rog, even as a teenager, still sort of hug me as long as no one is looking? I know I'm a lot closer to my children than I was to my dad. It isn't a criticism, as the world was a very different place forty years ago, and it's not right to judge people using a different time's perspective.

To use a tired expression, the only constant is change. The children and I were the Three Musketeers, complete with Puss in Boots, for a year until Rose changed jobs, moved back to town and we reverted to week-on/week-off parenting. Although everything was going along splendidly, on reflection it had been a change that was best for everyone.

In my case it was now nice not being on duty all the time. I have new-found respect for single parents who fly solo. It was, though, a wonderful and life-changing time for me. I learnt about what's important in life and that being a parent isn't a sacrifice. I stopped minding that there was lots to do and it was all down to me. Work, study, fly home, check homework while cooking dinner, clean up, supervise teeth and bed and then, maybe, sit-down time. I just got on with it and found I could enjoy it as well. You're a long time dead so there's no point in missing the world.

Rose moving back meant work and study was going to be easier to organise and this had been a major concern. The reduced time meant I had taken on less consulting work and that resulted in less cash. It's a truism in business that cash is king. It's like blood, and bad things happen when there isn't enough of it in your system. In addition, my study meant that I needed to travel more to interview business strategists as they were hardly likely to come to me.

Rog and Liv were thrilled because they were going to get more Mum time. And a more relaxed Mum too who wasn't late and hassled after battling the Friday Wellington traffic. I know they loved being with me but it was at the expense of time with Mum in their own space and they needed that. Especially Liv, who occasionally became quite unsettled when Mum left on Sunday and required lots of hugs and even more chocolate. I had developed my feminine side but there was only so far I could go.

The children told me much later that going back to week-on/week-off meant that they got more *quality* time with me. This confused me at first but they explained that we now hung out together more in the weekends and could just be together. I'd missed that point. Even though I had the children for more time, the children were missing out on some of the fun time.

It delighted Rose as well. Apart from being liberated from a nasty commute, which must have been a curse, she'd been missing her time with the children. I can admit now that when she moved to Wellington I wondered if she was taking a backwards step and looking to enjoy more freedom in Wellington without the children. I was pleased to be wrong.

And that's where we are today. Two houses with similar but different flavours. I think it gives the children an opportunity to experience different ways of living and they'll work out for themselves which aspects they prefer as they mature. My house tends to be quieter with less visitors while Rose's frequently has friends and family staying over. Neither way is right or wrong, just different.

I'm pleased I had the chance to sail solo, though I would never have done it by choice. The children and I have always been close, but that time strengthened those bonds and we'll always be the Three Musketeers. It may not have been a far, far better thing that I did, than I have ever done; but it was pretty good.

Reflections

- The better you communicate with your ex, the easier everyone's lives will be. This is a key part of having a great relationship with your ex.
- Get the logistics between houses sorted out quickly. The goal is smooth and stress-free changeovers as that's in the best interests of your children.
- Don't sweat if your children seem to be transporting everything including the kitchen sink between houses. It will reduce, and in the short term it may make them feel more in control.
- Counselling isn't a soft option, even for Kiwi males. The most important aspect is to take in an open mind.

- *Using a notebook to exchange observations and concerns with your ex works well when communication is difficult.*
- *The more time you spend with your children will help build bonds that will endure for a lifetime. Be careful though – it has to be quality time.*
- *Take extra care when forwarding emails to your ex. Make sure you aren't putting your electronic foot in it.*

12. School Holidays

If there were no schools to take the children away from home part of the time, the insane asylums would be filled with mothers.
Edgar Watson Howe (novelist and editor, 1853–1937)

During the coffee break at a conference I was chatting with a group of people and I manoeuvred myself strategically so I was able to politely ask a noticeably attractive woman, 'So, what do you do?' I know it's a poor conversation starter but I'm not a natural social butterfly.

She replied, 'I'm a part-time teacher.'

'Really,' I said, 'I didn't think there was any such thing as a full-time teacher.'

Before I offend those in the teaching profession, I do have the utmost respect for teachers. I'm delighted that there are people who love, or at least endure, days on end with children of all ages. From kindergarten through to high school, I couldn't imagine a more testing work environment.

But …

Fourteen weeks a year of holidays, plus public holidays and teacher-only days. Wow, that's some down time. Rog's school regularly plans a teacher-only day on the Monday *after* the school holidays. Unless I'm missing something, school holidays are teacher-only days. It's obviously only a theory.

I have to scramble to make sure my children are cared for in the seemingly endless holidays. Life would be easier if I had the old-world luxury of a stay-at-home wife keeping the home fires burning, darning my socks and waiting for the children's return from school. Thankfully today's society is being dragged towards equality and few women are content with a role behind the often inflated ego of an ordinary man. It's certainly not a role I'll be encouraging Liv to settle for.

JUGGLING

I am luckier than many parents as being self-employed means that I'm in a position in which I can juggle the competing demands of work and home. Actually, strike the word 'lucky'. I've spent years studying and I've been running my own business for a decade. I agree with whoever said that luck comes to those who work hard and don't give up.

Even being self-employed, I'm still forced to write off most of the school holidays when the children are with me. That's seven weeks' worth (Rose and I share the holidays fifty-fifty) and school holidays come around brutally quickly. Using my nanny for the whole week is too expensive and so I block out the week. It's only when there are unavoidable work commitments that I drop the children at my mum's.

For those seven weeks I get little work done – and not working equals not earning. Add to that the increased costs required to keep the troops entertained and trips away and it can feel like my personal version of the Global Financial Crisis.

When the six-week Christmas break loomed in all its glory I was torn between having a summer break and progressing my study. I didn't want to shelve my research for half the holidays when I had the children, but I couldn't work from home as the software I was using was on my university computer. I was pondering this problem one night when I was struggling to go to sleep when, eureka, I came up with the solution: 'borrow' my university computer. Brilliant!

In bureaucracies there are two ways to do things. There's the official way, which results in frustration, and the easy way. I needed to complete an 'Uplift computer equipment' form and submit it to the administrator, who would coordinate approvals. As many of the university hierarchy were already on holiday my chances were slim. At the risk of offending more people, you can throw most academics into the part-time workforce.

The easy way was far simpler. I wandered into my office on a Sunday morning, with Rog and Liv to give me an innocent look, and some accomplices, and we picked up the computer and screen and uplifted it ourselves. Our action was in line with that common management saying: it's easier to ask for forgiveness than permission. I was therefore able to advance my study over the summer holidays when time allowed.

Did anyone notice my computer's absence for six weeks? Do you really have to ask?

The major barrier to getting anything meaningful done in the holidays is the constant interruptions. I read that managers get interrupted every seven minutes on average and it must be similar for parents when children are around. It feels far more frequently, especially if Liv is hungry.

'Dad, what's for: breakfast, lunch, dinner, dessert, morning tea … ?'

'Dad, can you: play, help, come here, get me a snack, pass that, hold this … ?'

'Dad, what are we doing: now, later, today, tomorrow, at lunchtime, after lunch … ?'

'Dad, I can't find my: top, shorts, socks, game, pencil, bangle, bat, brain, sandwich …'

It's endless. I learnt a handy lesson very early as a parent: when you're looking after your children and you expect to achieve a lot, you get frustrated and angry. If you expect to get nothing done and you actually achieve something, you feel elated. Managing your expectations helps.

There's also the tricky balance between not wanting the children on the computer all day and getting time for myself. I'm sure that if left unchecked Rog would stay on his computer or Xbox constantly if he didn't need to eat or attend to the occasional call of nature. When he's engrossed in a game, Rog hangs on for as long as humanly possible and then sprints to the toilet. Good job we have two – otherwise it could end badly.

It isn't because I don't want to spend time with the children during the holidays. I love hanging out or tripping around with them, it's great fun. But balancing work and holidays can be a trial. I know there are other options available, such as holiday programmes, which would allow me a full work day. However, Rog and Liv experienced one once, threatened rebellion and refused to attend the last day. This forced Rose, who equally doesn't have a sock-darning partner, to take the day off. I've subsequently shied away from using them, though I'm sure there are good ones around. Maybe Rose was just unlucky.

Despite the evidence and my own experience, I still optimistically plan to get lots of work and study done. I bring it home in folders which mainly sit in my office taunting me. There are periods of time when I can strike, usually early morning or late in the evening. It has to be quite late now as the children's bedtime has extended as they've grown. I do miss the days of afternoon naps and having my angels asleep by 7.30pm. Studying requires long periods of uninterrupted concentration and so early in the morning before they're awake is ideal. When they arise, bedraggled and enquiring about breakfast, I change to work tasks and try ignore them for as long as possible.

Public holidays present a similar, albeit briefer, challenge. They certainly lose their gloss when you don't get paid. So it's difficult to join in the excited chatter about the long weekend. I'm usually planning on doing what I would've done anyway except there'll be nobody else in the building. As public holidays approach I secretly hope they fall when the children are at Rose's, and I reckon she does the same.

Then there are all those 'special' days such as Mother's Day, Father's Day, Valentine's Day, Easter and Christmas. They're just commercial traps. Does anyone eat hot cross buns and chocolate only at Easter, or wait until Valentine's Day to show affection? I make an effort for the children, I'm not the Grinch I make out, but they're used to my relaxed view that celebrating near the date is okay. I once gave my brother his birthday present six months late – he probably thought I'd forgotten.

Rose loves special days and she and the children celebrate with gusto. This works for us both and on one occasion allowed me the opportunity to head to the UK for Christmas without them. I'd taken them with me previously but so that I could leave with a clear conscience, I bribed them with the promise of spectacular presents on my return. They were more than happy with that – effectively it meant two Christmases. I kept my promise and bought more presents than I should have, mainly to allay any leftover guilt. It was my first Christmas without them but I needn't have worried, they'd survived fine and were thrilled to dive into Christmas take two.

UP, UP AND AWAY

One memorable present I bought for Rog was a solar airship from the London Science Museum. Rog was keen to test out its capabilities, though the instructions said – in fact they stressed – that the airship should be flown only on windless days. In Palmerston North they're reasonably rare, even in summer, and it took a few days of patience before the day dawned bright, sunny and calm. After breakfast the children and I headed to the school field for its inaugural flight.

Like most toys, the appearance of the airship wasn't as thrilling as it looked on the package but it was still impressive. It was a colossal thin, black polythene tube that, once inflated, used the sun to heat the trapped air allowing it to soar skywards. It was stopped from escaping by a string attached like a kite.

As we readied the airship for flight I noticed that the breeze was freshening. This made things tricky but eventually we got it inflated. The sun started doing its job and we waited for the airship to fulfil its destiny and fly. Unfortunately, all it managed was to writhe barely off the ground like a giant black sausage on a barbeque. The day was already hot and it wasn't a lack of solar power that was thwarting its flight. Rog and Liv danced delightedly around it while I waited and pondered.

After half an hour the airship's and my limit had been reached. I noticed a slight tear in the tube and so I decided we should deflate it and take it home for rest and repair. The children grabbed their scooters, my plan B, and we headed to the tennis courts with the airship in tow.

'How are we going to deflate it?' Rog asked seriously.

'I'm going to attach it to the fence and let it deflate itself.'

I secured it to the wire-netting fence that surrounded the tennis courts by pushing the handle through the wire netting.

'I thought you said you were going to tie it?'

'I said attach. If the airship tries to escape … ,' and I demonstrated by tugging on the string that the handle couldn't get back through the fence. It was like a lobster trap.

'That's clever, Dad.'

I smiled and he ran off with his scooter to join Liv while I lay down in the sun. I'd only been back in the country for a few days and I felt like I was still high above the Pacific. I could hear the children playing happily and stretched out hoping to have a quick nap.

No sooner than I had closed my eyes when I heard Rog yelling out in alarm. My brain was still foggy and it took a moment to register that the breeze had amazingly freed the airship. Really? I watched it gently writhing slowly across the playing field in disbelief. I struggled to my feet and stumbled into a jog to retrieve and re-incarcerate the rogue airship. It hadn't got higher than a couple of metres and it had a tear in it, so I assumed it wasn't going anywhere fast.

I was wrong.

As I closed the gap on the airship it was though it sensed danger and started to climb. Three metres. Four metres. Recognising the impending disaster I accelerated, but by the time I caught up with it its dangling kite handle was out of reach. I ran along underneath waiting, and hoping, for it to descend but it had other plans. Ten, fifteen, twenty metres … Halfway across the field, and as inconceivable as it seemed, it wasn't coming down. In fact it was still climbing and wriggling delightedly in its new-found freedom. I stopped and was joined by Rog and Liv who had abandoned their scooters and joined the chase. We watched it soar higher and higher, over the trees, out of sight and away to far-off places.

I was at a loss for words and Rog was far from impressed. We followed what I calculated to be its likely flight path but it was a futile effort. Like the *Titanic*, it hadn't survived its maiden voyage and we never saw it again. I half expected to hear on the evening news that air travel around Palmerston North had been disrupted by an unidentified flying sausage. Rog reminded me for weeks that I owed him a solar airship the next time I was in London. I still owe it to him and he won't forget. If I mention the airship today his face instantly sours. Maybe I'll make it a twenty-first birthday present …

THE CHIEF ENTERTAINMENT OFFICER

It seems logical that looking after one child would be easier than two but it's completely the opposite. When my children are together they play, work out games and generally keep each other amused. Yes, they have the odd dust-up but that just comes with the territory. They can play with the box of Hot Wheels cars and track for hours, and now they're older, with their interests separating, they play multi-player computer games together. When one is away the difference is striking because all the attention is focused back on me. It's fair enough and we do have fun, but it means I achieve far less than I hope or plan.

12. School Holidays

Looking after Rog and Liv in the holidays has become easier as they've grown. They love sleeping in, pottering around the house, playing on their computers, watching TV and generally staying in their pyjamas all day. That suits me down to the ground. They're aware, because I keep telling them, that I'm not the chief entertainment officer, at least not all the time. If they get too ratty with each other, or with me, I say loudly, 'Next holidays I'll probably have to consider a holiday programme, at least for my most annoying child.' They know I'm all talk, but they slink away into the shadows – for a while.

When we're holidaying at home I like to get the children out of the house at least once a day. Going for a walk is a favourite of mine. At first their facial expressions suggest a distinct lack of keenness, though I suspect they like them once we are underway. The bonus with walking is I get the chance to chat to them about whatever comes to mind. I love finding out what's going on inside their heads. It's often hard to fathom, but it's always interesting. Occasionally, mainly from Liv whom Rog nicknamed 'Bean-spiller', I may get a titbit or two of gossip. This was sometimes valuable in the early days when Rose and I kept our cards close to our chest.

The shortest walk is around the block for an ice cream or down to the lagoon to feed the ducks. The longest walk we tackle is around the nearby gorge called, unsurprisingly, the gorge walk. Suggesting this walk brings out facial expressions in the children ranging from bewilderment to resignation. This may be due to the time I playfully took a couple of short cuts and we missed our turn-off. The result was an extra half hour back-tracking. As we slogged our way back up the hill we had recently descended, I explained to them that we'd all learned a valuable lesson about sticking to the track and how this may save their lives one day. They weren't fooled or impressed, especially Liv who was busting for number twos. I tried to convince her that finding a quiet place and using some soft, luxuriant ferns was what you did in the bush. She was having none of it. Clearly she's going to be a metro girl.

The school holidays are fun, but like parents across the globe I'm pleased to see the end of them. As the children drag themselves back to school, the majority of parents high five quietly out of sight. This is because the real world, that hungry furnace that demands time and money, has been put on hold and I now have to sprint to catch up. With the children back at school I jump back on the economic treadmill, whether I want to or not.

The school system may not have changed for over a century but the world certainly has. Therefore I feel duty bound to update the quote from Edgar Watson Howe that started this chapter. I have made it both politically correct and applicable for today, albeit a tad clumsy:

> *If there were no schools to take the children away from home part of the time, the psychiatric hospitals would be filled with a mix of married and single, heterosexual and homosexual, mothers, fathers, family, whanau and other primary care-givers.*

Reflections

- The antiquated school system was not designed with you and your children's life in mind. You have to set up your own systems and processes to make it work smoothly.
- Make sure you plan your holidays to suit everyone and not only work for you.
- When you're looking after your children don't expect to get any work done and you'll be delighted if you do.
- When you attach a kite to a fence, attach it. Boys, in particular, have memories like elephants.
- If you're trying to make a good impression with an attractive teacher, tact is required around the hours they work.
- If you find yourself at home with your children in the holidays, just go with the flow and have fun. Soon your children won't be children.

13. A Woman's Touch

If you want a golden rule that will fit everything, this is it: Have nothing in your house that you do not know to be useful or believe to be beautiful.
William Morris (designer, writer and activist, 1834–96)

When I transformed from a married man into a single parent I didn't realise I was embarking on a rare social experiment – the creation of a functioning family environment devoid of a woman's touch. Cathy let me know what changes she thought needed to be made but I didn't change anything apart from her insistence that I put locks on the toilet doors. The locks apart, my home has been designed and decorated with only this male's touch.

I tried to call this chapter something else as I thought the term 'a woman's touch' sounded sexist, but nothing else encapsulated the concept as well as that phrase. It isn't employed in a derogatory sense, it's more a compliment, and I'm using the phrase to convey the ability to bring together style, fashion and functionality.

I used the term 'designed' but that's probably an over-statement. 'Opportunistic' is maybe a more apt description of my home's unique look and feel. After I moved in there was little interior decorating that needed to be done and I only painted Liv's room because she objected to the pale-blue colour. I bought furniture over the next two months, keeping to a solid wood theme, native rimu where possible. I added art to the walls and luxuriated in buying what I liked. Art is very individualistic and hanging prints of Dali and Escher felt liberating. Every knick-knack that wasn't a gift or made by the children, along with the extensive range of pot plants, have all been lovingly selected and positioned by me.

The outdoor surrounds also bear my signature and here I was more ruthless. I took out a number of trees that looked out of control and generally expanded the size of the lawn for backyard cricket, tennis and soccer. I bought some second-hand outdoor furniture and used it to establish a compact breakfast area on the veranda and an outdoor setting in the backyard – though they aren't used that frequently. Even less often since the two-seater collapsed under the weight of an unlucky guest.

Since the initial burst of activity after moving in I've only tinkered, leaving the house and surrounds a product of my male sense of fashion and function. I have an idea of the image that is produced – guests who are aware of my marital circumstances are often genuinely surprised when they arrive.

'Wow, this is really nice,' a university colleague remarked when borrowing a textbook.

'What did you expect?'

'I don't know, something like your office, I guess. This seems, well … normal.'

I confess my office is a tip but when you're studying you pile things on every flat surface. My home is different because it's not solely for me, it's a family home.

THE SALAD SERVERS

The inspiration for this chapter came from left field. I was oblivious to the fact that my home had a masculine feel until one Father's Day Rog, twelve at the time, bought me a set of salad servers. Nothing unusual about that, I'm sure they're a common present. The surprise came when I went to put them away and discovered that I didn't own a set of salad servers.

Had you asked me how many salad servers I owned before that Father's Day, I would have said at least two, maybe three. That was my brain reclaiming items long ago left behind in our marital kitchen. Of greater concern was that for over five years I'd obviously never needed to call on the service of salad servers. That just couldn't be right.

Please don't think that means my children and I haven't had a salad in five years. We have, but for the three of us it's easier to make it directly on the plates rather than in a salad bowl, which just creates one more dish to be washed. This method works well, especially for Liv who, unless salad is directly applied, is unlikely to let it grace her plate. Even then she gives it a token effort and treats it as though it will multiply if she touches it too much. I resort to the threat of withholding dessert unless she makes a *decent* attempt at the greenery and that results in a debate about what constitutes a decent attempt. She's getting better, slowly.

You may be wondering what I do when I have friends over for refined and elaborate dinner parties or barbeques. 'I don't' is the short answer. Throwing or attending dinner parties are seldom on the dance card of this single dad. I've hosted a few barbeques but zero dinner parties. My friend Simon popped over once for dinner but he brought fish and chips with him and I supplied the beer. Salad never featured on the menu or in conversation. I don't count that as a dinner party.

I realise that this paints me in a forlorn and lonely light, but it's mainly due to the mechanics of a week-on/week-off lifestyle. When the children are here the weeks are hectic. Inviting people over isn't on the radar until Saturday, by which time it's too late. Sunday evening they go to Rose's. Maybe it's just me, but being by myself does not instantly start me wondering who to invite over next weekend and what I can cook. Quite the contrary.

Dinner parties are also social events that traditionally revolve around couples or via work colleagues. Once you've been a guest you feel obliged to reciprocate, and the cycle commences. As I'm single and self-employed, the opportunities are limited. It isn't that I don't like dinner parties, I do. But there are people who consider being single as an illness to be cured and make dinner parties awkward first dates. Thankfully I don't have friends like that and I haven't, at least yet, found myself the subject of someone's well-intentioned match-making experiment.

Re-reading and editing the previous paragraphs, for the umpteenth time which is the writing process, has made me wonder whether I've become too reclusive. Introspective writing, and its associated thinking, has a tendency to ask questions that you were blissfully unaware needed asking. While you may have an inkling that there are areas in your life that may benefit from attention, they're like old clothes in the wardrobe – out of sight, out of mind. It's when they're brought into stark clarity that you see them in their true light. And once you're aware, it's impossible to become unaware.

The arrival of salad servers motivated me to look around my home with a critical eye, a feminine eye. I asked myself the question – what does my home look like to the rest of the world? What does it say about me? That's something I'm sure most males seldom do because, let's face it, we don't really care. We are content leaving that question to our significant other! At the very least, though, I was curious.

On first inspection everything looked satisfactory, typical even. I began to think that the salad servers may be an aberration. It wasn't until I looked harder that I started to understand that the concept of a woman's touch is subtle and in the details. It's making sure the carpets and curtains match. Having lamps and a lighting scheme that blend in – or simply being aware that having a lighting scheme is a good place to start.

This explains why one of the tasks many people dive into when moving into a new house is replacing carpets, curtains or lighting. This was lost on me as I've been in this house for over seven years and the carpets, curtains and lighting have remained untouched. That would indicate to me that they must blend in, or I would have noticed. Right? Unfortunately I get the feeling that if you don't notice and act straight away, you never will. Over time everything becomes part of the background. It's similar to being in a new country where initially everything is new and fascinating – 'Wow, look at these double decker buses.' A few weeks later it dissolves into the mundane – 'The bloody bus is late. Again.'

If you cast a cursory glance around my house you could be forgiven for thinking fashion is on an equal footing. But, as I said, the absence of a woman's touch is in the detail. I performed a few critical circuits of my house and I started to see things of which I was previously blissfully ignorant. For example, nearly every lampshade is different. I don't know if that's wonderfully eclectic or simply a mishmash.

In my bedroom there's no mirror. The reason for this is that after seven years clearly I don't need one. After my usual morning shower, if I think it's necessary I can check myself in the bathroom mirror. But there isn't much in a grooming sense that requires feedback. How I emerge from the shower is pretty much as good as I'm going to get.

Once dressed, I have no need of a full-length mirror to make sure my shoes go with my suit. They either have or haven't, with minor variations, for years. There is, I grant you, the odd occasion when I do want to see myself in all my glory. I do this by using the full-length mirror in Liv's room, which I installed as I thought she should have one. Rog doesn't have a mirror and has never asked for one. I think this is because he's unaware he needs one, though this may change as his teenage years gather momentum.

When I use Liv's full-length mirror it requires two views as it's a full-length mirror for a seven-year-old. I view the top half by kneeling in front of the mirror and then stand to view the bottom half. It's a cursory glance at best, if I'm honest. The chances of changing clothes based on this feedback are slim — though it has been known.

There are more effective ways than a mirror of receiving feedback about how you look and whether you're putting on weight. Friends, like my brutally honest student colleagues, are ideal.

'Did you have a good break over summer?' Uri asked.

'Yep. I managed to forget all about study and caught up on doing nothing,' I replied.

'We thought so. You are looking fatter in the face.'

We thought so. They'd obviously all noticed and discussed my weight increase but it wasn't said with any malice, just as a fact. You've put on weight, you munter.

I was aware I'd put on a few kilos that summer as on my return to work my suit trousers felt overly snug. Confirmation came violently one morning when I bent down to retrieve my car keys. The sound was like a zipper being undone and I was suddenly aware that the morning breeze was on the cool side. I retreated inside without a word, leaving the waiting children perplexed. Thankfully I have a spare suit. When I reappeared at the front door, I held up my trousers to demonstrate what had happened.

'What the — that's the biggest rip I've ever seen,' Liv said wide-eyed. 'What a munter.' It was impressive.

KIWI INGENUITY

A functional feature, unlikely to be a fixture in many bedrooms, is an ironing board. It isn't the ironing board per se, it's the fact it's been permanently erected for years and performs a similar function to a chest of drawers, without the drawers. It's seldom used for ironing, though it was initially erected for this purpose, with business shirts the major exception. It's now a suitable place to put clothes when they're between being put away, as well as the washing basket.

Usually it's piled with sweatshirts, track pants and casual shirts waiting for a second wear. I suspect style would dictate another approach, but the ironing board serves admirably and it's able to be cleared in seconds if required.

After writing the last paragraph I decided that a permanently erected ironing board wasn't the look I wanted to portray and so I took it down, put it away and deleted the paragraph. However, without it I started copying Liv and using the floordrobe. It was back within a few days and the paragraph reinstated. I could buy a chair or something similar to replace the ironing board but that, I think, illustrates my point.

In terms of décor and taste the children's rooms seem perfect. To get them feeling snug only required a parent's touch, which I have in spades. The only aspect that's questionable is their wardrobes, or to be more accurate the lack of them. When I bought the house there were two plastic, skeletal, stand-alone wardrobes which I immediately ditched. Even I could detect they were unsightly and I would have paid someone to take them away but I sold them on TradeMe (the New Zealand equivalent of Ebay) and got a bonus $20.

For the next few years wardrobing wasn't a problem as the children had little that needed hanging except for coats and I'd acquired a stylish, wooden coat rack for that purpose. It was the arrival of school uniforms that necessitated a change in their wardrobing requirements.

The children and I went to a local furniture shop and discovered that stand-alone wardrobes were universally ugly and expensive. I had in mind a sleek, modern, bird-like form in steel for about $50. The best of an average lot, which was also the cheapest, wasn't in stock and would take two weeks to arrive. In my typical style I'd left it until school was about to start, so we returned home empty handed. I got the feeling that Rog and Liv couldn't have cared less but I was determined that they have somewhere to hang their school uniform. Otherwise they would happily ditch them on the floor without a second thought.

While putting Liv to bed that night I noticed a chain that was fixed across the corner of her room. It was part of a hammock used to display her stuffed teddies and along the chain she had hung various teddy bears. Hung in a nice decorative way, that is, rather than a teddy bear horror show.

'Why don't we hang your clothes from that?' I asked, motioning towards the corner.

Liv frowned, considering the option.

'What about the teddies?'

'We can make a small gap. You haven't got that many clothes that need hanging up.'

Liv continued to frown.

'Yeah,' she said suddenly, bursting into a smile.

Brilliant. One down and at zero cost.

I strolled confidently into Rog's room, where I wasn't so lucky. There was nothing that resembled a place that could accommodate hanging clothes. But I wasn't to be defeated and the next day I bought a wardrobe rail and secured it with picture hanging wire to the top of his chest of drawers. It wasn't my prettiest work, but it was effective. Rog's clothes could all be accommodated and kept off the floor. Just. Rog wasn't yet a strapping six-footer and the school uniform dictated short pants.

There was an alarming health and safety issue with this arrangement as the rail projected towards his bedroom door at goolie height. This was a significant concern for Rog and me but so far only Liv has blundered on to it with her stomach. Rog and I were in hysterics as she yelled, 'Your wardrobe solution gutsed me!'

I managed to find wardrobing solutions for both children, and all for $7.50. That is Kiwi ingenuity at its finest. The solutions are, I admit, definitely well towards the useful side of William Morris's golden rule that started this chapter.

THE KITCHEN

My kitchen is okay, though function has whopped style here. The stove and the previously described bungee cord and the dishwasher's need of a bamboo pole being the two most obvious examples. The bungee cord may be a negative in terms of style but I've never thought that any stove possesses beauty.

The fridge, on the other hand, is functional and has a beauty the stove will never have. The fridge contains items that can be consumed immediately. To acquire this beauty the stove needs to be able to present the piping hot soup or lightly seared orange roughy and couscous ready for the person who opens the door. This level of technology would benefit humanity by eliminating the need for cooking shows and celebrity chefs.

My kitchen lacks the gadgets that someone with a greater affinity for cooking would possess. It has all the basics needed for preparing and cooking mainstream dishes, but few of the devices dreamt up by chefs looking to make money and avoid cooking. If I had to julienne something or someone I'd be likely to surprise and disappoint them, probably in that order.

The crockery and cutlery are all plain and unexciting but functional. Similar are the glasses, which are in uninspiring depleted sets. I wouldn't call them cheap but they are low middle-of-the-road. They're there primarily to be useful and not beautiful. If I desired classier glasses or plates, which I don't, then I would happily pay a lot more. They would get broken by myself and the children in exactly the same way as the current ones do, except I'd get more irate. I'm saving money and reducing stress; it's a bargain. I'm sure there'll be a time and place for classier kitchen items. Maybe.

The final area of note, as Liv marches towards her teenage years, is the sparseness of the bathroom. I don't have screeds of liquids and potions dotted on every available surface. In fact Cathy's left behind more items than I had in the first place. One item I have recently invested in for Liv is a hair dryer. For years I convinced her that the fan heater in her room does exactly the same job, which it does, but the functional argument was wearing pretty thin. Added to that was the sight of Liv drying her hair while looking as if she was listening to a boom box wasn't great.

If I had to give my home an overall mark for style and beauty as opposed to functionality, I would award the mark I consistently received at school, B- with the comment 'Could do better if he applied himself'. In saying that, writing this chapter wasn't the revelation I thought it might be. I thought the lack of a woman's touch was going to stand out like a sore thumb, but apart from a few areas my home is normal. Leaving the kitchen aside, my home has a look and feel that would be similar to the majority of family homes. Including those that have a critical feminine eye.

The most important element in my home that bucks the function over fashion trend is my children. They *must* be beautiful, and they are, as most of the time they aren't that useful. Though they have their moments.

Reflections

- The abundance or absence of salad servers is a useful measure of the state of your house on the fashion/function continuum.
- It pays to assess your home from time to time with a critical eye to make sure function hasn't dominated style to an embarrassing level. You simply stop seeing after a while.
- As a single parent it is easy to become isolated and you need to be proactive to counter this.
- You don't have to spend lots of money to add touches of style to your home. Art prints and pot plants worked for me.
- Mirrors appear to be optional accessories in a male world. Ironing boards, however, are a little-known bedroom accessory.

14. Fitness and Fatness

I spent my whole single life trying to be thin just to find someone who'd love me once I got fat.
Stephanie Klein (writer)

We're besieged during our waking hours by the weight-loss industry looking to increase their sizeable profits. Most of their messages are subtle, though some are brick-like in their bluntness. The endless stream of perfect bodies used in marketing and entertainment subliminally impresses upon us that this is what you, and your partner, should be aspiring to look like. Have you ever made the mistake of suggesting that your partner may need to lose some weight or focus on exercise? I have. Once. That cooled the temperature in the room pretty damn quick and it didn't warm again for days.

I'm far from obsessed with my fitness and weight but I prefer feeling fit and trim, or at least trimish. But knowing that your outward appearance has little to do with you as a person doesn't help me when someone gives me the once-over. As a species humans put a lot of emphasis, and can tell a lot, from that quick once-over. It's partly defensive, in that we're trying to work out if this person is dangerous or we're likely to be eaten. It is also, of course, partly procreative as we try to ascertain if this is an opportunity to help the species survive, adapt and prosper through the sharing of genetic code (although we seldom think of it in quite those terms). It is, however, hard to fight thousands of years of evolutionary fine tuning.

As a dad, and more particularly a single dad, I have a few reasons for keeping fit.

First is to simply keep up with Rog and Liv. Whether it's tennis, cricket, swimming, volleyball or soccer, I like to be able to play and practise with them as well as take part in events that include parents. Liv and I played in a parent-child tennis tournament, and while we didn't win we had fun. I'm also keen for the chance to play against Rog in a cricket match one day. I know he would love to clout me for a four or a six. I'd never hear the end of it.

Second, image and brand are important in business. As I'm self-employed, I represent myself. Wearing a suit and being presentable are part of the business world. It's interesting that research from two Australian universities has shown that good-looking male workers can earn 20 per cent more than their plainer colleagues. In true Australian style they also reported that outright ugliness can reduce a man's earnings by 26 per cent. If looking good helps me earn more money, that's great. I learnt at the start of my businesses career to never say 'It's not the money'.

The final reason is that there have been periods when my long-distance relationship has been too complex and I've found myself single. In an available state, if I'm at a party (rare), the pub (not so rare) or a work situation (common), the reaction I'd like to get from a female once-over is 'Cor, I'd do him!' A UK article I saw describing the experiences of middle-aged females on the dating scene slated the appearance, teeth, hygiene and conversational ability of single males in my age range. In many respects that's great. It sounds like the majority of people out there make me look good. Still, I'd like to aim higher.

CALORIES IN

To keep trim, fit and healthy I've developed a range of strategies that seem to work for me and my single-dad lifestyle. I recently picked up some sound advice while watching a televised debate on weight loss. A scientist was explaining how the human body is a thermodynamic system in which the key equation for weight gain or loss is energy in and energy out. If you consume more calories than you expend, the surplus calories are stored as fat. Conversely, expend more than you consume and your body burns the stored fat. I found this logic simple and it seemed to mirror reality. If you eat like a horse then there's a good chance you'll look like a horse, at least from the rear!

This logic also eliminated the need for the stupid organic, hydroponic, low-carb, low-fat and low-taste diets which are guaranteed to drive you to steak, ale and chips within thirty-six hours. All I had to do was watch what I ate (calories in) and exercised sufficiently (calories out). All calories aren't the same, though, and you need to eat a balanced diet. Consuming all your calories through alcohol and pizza or McDonald's doesn't work, despite what their advertising may say. Morgan Spurlock of *Supersize Me* fame tried this approach, much to the detriment of his health.

I found that eating healthy wasn't that hard during the weeks when I have the children. I ensure they eat a healthy, balanced diet and therefore I do too. I give them a light breakfast of toast, cereal or croissants and I occasionally make pancakes as they are Liv's favourite. A healthy lunch consisting of a sandwich, cereal bar, fruit and, as we aren't saints, chips and biscuits. Dinner is your standard meal of meat and two veg or a pasta dish. I would happily skip dessert as, unlike Rog and Liv, I haven't a sweet tooth. But I ensure my rabble are kept from rioting by providing them with dessert. Cut-up fruit and chocolate dipping sauce are a cunning way to make half the dessert healthy.

Watching what I eat and, more importantly, what I drink I find tougher when I'm alone because I don't have to practise what I preach. I regularly skip breakfast and just have coffee. There is zero chance of making lunch when I don't have to make the children's. I dislike making lunches to the point that one of the blessings of the school holidays is their absence. For lunch, cafés or the university student centre are my usual targets. The student centre has a range of healthy options, but chicken and chips or a Chinese boxed take-out are hard to resist. Although I dislike cooking for one, I make an effort with dinner most nights balanced with the odd visit to my Mum's and the local kebab shop. I can exercise more in my weeks without the children and I think that helps keep me in balance, though beer can tip the scales.

Alcohol, specifically beer, is my biggest weakness when it comes to calories in and a more virtuous lifestyle. It's unfortunate, even outrageous, that a small bottle of beer has 300 calories. There are those lucky people who just have *a* beer but that's usually not me and so my calorie intake can rapidly increase in multiples of 300. Then there's the well-known fact that beer hones your appetite razor-sharp. It's a bad combination and can result in the children's stash of sweets being seen as fair game post-dinner. I replace the items ransacked so the children don't miss out and there's no evidence of my sugar splurge.

My stance regarding food is pretty relaxed. I try to eat healthily, but if I splurge on something I try to fit in an extra gym session as penance. During our marriage Rose convinced me to try the 'Body for Life' programme with her. I found that the exercise regime made sense but the diet suggestions were over the top. I couldn't understand the rationale of having an omelette with only the white of the egg. That's not the way nature intended the world to work. Rose's anaemic omelette looked and tasted horrible. I took the muttered lack of commitment comments with my yellow and tasty omelette. I even added contraband items like butter and cheese when she wasn't watching.

A casual approach to dieting is sensible and more workable for me in the long run. Besides, I haven't heard any evidence that fad diets are effective for long-term weight loss. In fact a colleague who studies the weight-loss industry tells me that technically the term for them should be bollocks. That makes sense because if there was a sure dieting method then it would now be common knowledge. They may help you shed a few kilos before summer but they'll be back by winter with a couple of friends for good measure. Given that, and the clinically proven fact that people on diets end up miserable gits, I thought a greater focus on the calories-out side of the equation made sense: exercise.

CALORIES OUT

I like exercise and I don't find it a chore, though it's not a pleasure either. During the weeks by myself I plan a lot of exercise but in the weeks with the children it's logistically harder. I did set up a home gym in the garage, one of my few possessions from the separation. I tried using it during these weeks but it now sits with an impressive layer of dust covering it. There's a good reason for that which I will get to shortly.

My preference is to attend karate and exercise classes. They are tough and sometimes I have to drag myself there with a constant dialogue in my head telling me to head home and put my feet up, you deserve it today. I have been known to drive to and past the dojo or gym on cold, wintery nights. Those occasions are rare and I'm usually pretty bouncy on the way in. I'm not so bouncy on the way out, more *draggy*.

When I started karate and attending gym classes I started taking more interest in my weight as the most obvious indicator of improvement. After six weeks of diligent training and watching my diet I was clearly getting fitter as I didn't feel like dying after every session. But, disappointingly, according to the scales I was getting fatter. Somehow a couple of extra kilos had got under my skin in more ways than one.

I realised that this situation was being caused by two related phenomena. First, as you exercise you add muscle which is more dense than fat. It isn't heavier, as a kilo of muscle equals a kilo of fat, but the same mass of muscle weighs more than the equivalent mass of fat. I was replacing fat with muscle and it was natural my weight would increase. I liked this affirming, scientific explanation.

However, it's the second factor that contains the 'gotcha'. My focus on exercise had me starting to believe my own bullshit. I convinced myself, at least subconsciously, that I can consume as many calories as I like because my body needs the fuel. My finely tuned athletic body could eat, drink and be merry. Hence the double whammy – you add muscle and you don't lose much fat. Damn. I needed to exercise something else, that most difficult and painful word, moderation. It was this that allowed me to start turning into an Adonis. Well, at least a pale, middle-aged Kiwi version.

The final piece of the puzzle regarding exercise was identifying the level of intensity I needed to reach during exercise. No rocket science was required, it was simply the amount of sweat I produced. I left karate in a sweat-soaked *gi* and absolutely knackered. I was, however, leaving the gym, before I started attending the classes, with a spring in my step in clothes that I could wear again (decency and courtesy being the only barrier to actually doing this).

The difference was entirely down to having an instructor. The karate sensei, or teacher, made sure we worked intensely for the entire session. You aren't even allowed off the mat for water, it's part of the tradition and discipline. I found it impossible to capture the same level of intensity in the gym and after about half an hour I was bored and ready to stop. I abandoned the treadmill, cross trainers, exercycles and weights and decided to try instead one of the instructor-led fitness classes. I'd been doing karate for a few years and thought that while the classes would be more intense than the gym, they would be a walk in the park compared to karate. Body Attack immediately changed my mind.

It would have been more accurate to call it Body Massacre and it should come with a warning for cocky, middle-aged men who believe they're fit. After my first class I suffered for the next few days. I couldn't bend down to pick up the ball when I was coaching Rog's cricket team. When it came near me I kicked it to the nearest child pretending it was the cool thing to do. The intensity generated in the class was similar to karate because the instructor set a breakneck let's-all-die-together pace. While there are low-intensity options, and you can take a break at any time, the pumping music and enthusiastic instructor keep you striving to maintain the pace. This results in you finishing the class drenched in sweat but feeling good. I was hooked and became a regular attendee at Body Attack, Body Step and Body Combat. This is the reason my home gym sits idly gathering dust. I equally can't replicate the enthusiasm and intensity required in my garage.

Lyn, my student colleague, and I became gym buddies. Having someone to go with makes it harder to bunk off on cold nights. I admired the fact that she wasn't put off going even though her religion meant she had to have no bare skin showing other than her face: track pants, long-sleeved shirt and a head scarf during sessions in the summer that left those of us in shorts and a T-shirt sweating like pigs.

EXERCISING WITH THE CHILDREN

I like to add exercise into my day by getting out and about with the children. I see parents at the pool reading and/or eating while their children swim. Not me, I'm in the pool too. Try it next time. Jump in with them and splash about, it's more fun for everyone. You get to act like a kid again and it adds exercise to your day.

The children and I often hire an inner tube and then battle over the right to lie on it spread-eagled until we are exhausted. I like to go early in the morning so the pool isn't crowded, but we still attract disapproving looks when we get in the way of adults who are trying to swim lengths. I smile apologetically but insincerely and have to bite my tongue to avoid pointing out that we are in the family pool, not the lengths pool. The clue is surely in the names.

Walking, while unlikely to change your shape much, is a pleasant evening activity in summer. I sometimes sweeten the deal by bribing Rog and Liv with the promise of ice cream, though this adds exercise into dessert.

They often rode their scooters, until they outgrew them, while I jogged or walked briskly. Liv briefly upgraded to a ripstick, which appears to defy many known laws of physics – a single wheel on the front and back of a skateboard that can twist in the middle. It looks impossible, but bored-looking children wiggle past on their way to school. Liv was pretty good on one and would wiggle her way up and down the street with ease. I tried it once and managed a few metres before ending up on my backside, much to my children's delight. Thankfully it wasn't captured on camera where I could have gone viral.

During our walks I have to keep a wary eye where I step as my left ankle rolls easily, the result of a bad sprain at karate. When it happens I usually lurch sharply left and hit the deck with a cry of pain and numerous, unavoidable swear words. I have twisted my ankle in this manner in numerous settings – in the PhD lab where everyone thought that was hilarious, on the cobblestones of the Seine as one cobblestone was missing, and at various other places.

One memorable time my ankle betrayed me was when the children and I were walking on a section of bush walk. There were a lot of tree roots criss-crossing the path and I warned them to be careful. The path was narrow but my sociable little Liv, nine at the time, insisted on walking next to me and holding my hand. Suddenly I felt the familiar rush of pain as I trod on one of the roots I was hoping to avoid.

My left ankle gave way and I yawed violently left, off the path and down the bank. I let Liv's hand go so I didn't drag her with me and slid head first towards an unpleasant-looking swamp. It wasn't a life-threatening situation, just poise and pride denting. I could hear Liv yelling in my wake, 'DDDAAADDDYYY'. I desperately grabbed bushes and clumps of grass, trying to slow my momentum. I clawed myself to a halt a metre or two before the dark and noxious-smelling muck. Liv was up on the bank with wide eyes. Rog, who had been walking ahead, came back to aid in my rescue. I was in an inverted heap, dry, relatively clean and laughing. My ankle wasn't badly hurt, it never is, and once I struggled back to the path we carried on this time in single file.

Liv has a curious knack of being in the thick of things on our walks. When she was seven she had to scooter home from the ducks with only one gumboot. Rog and I were busy feeding the ducks when I glanced over and saw Liv looking puzzled in one gumboot and one sock. I looked around and couldn't see the other gumboot, only Liv looking sorry for herself. After some gentle cajoling it emerged that she'd been chasing a duck and went to give it 'a friendly kick' as it had been pecking other ducks. Unfortunately her gumboot had flown off and into the lagoon, never to be seen again.

Liv, who loves animals and is a gentle soul, can be a bit mischievous like that. I have a photo of her when she was three sitting on a bench with one of our cats, Flecky, in front of her. Flecky quite rightly has a concerned look on her face as Liv's gumboot is high over her tail. Her kick had missed by a proverbial whisker.

Staying active and healthy allows me to keep up to the required pace of my single-dad lifestyle. Whether it's being able to charge around with my children who get faster every day, get through my days with a spring in my step, enhance my brand image and cash flow, or allow for hard-wired snap judgements to go my way, I will continue to eat healthily, sweat, strain and run away from the more flabby and sickly person stalking me.

Reflections

- Being fit and healthy when you're a single parent lets you keep up with your children and may get you a second glance.
- With regards to your weight, keep it simple. Eat as healthily as possible and exercise as much as you can while keeping it enjoyable. Don't buy into the diet fads, which only reduce your bank balance.
- You have to be more disciplined regarding diet and alcohol when the children aren't around.
- Unless you're incredibly self-motivated, fitness classes should help you get to a higher level of exercise intensity and make you sweat. It feels great afterwards.
- Just because you are exercising it doesn't mean you can now consume the calories of an elephant, unless you want to look like a reasonably fit elephant.
- Get into the pool with your children. It's great fun and burns calories.
- Incorporating exercise such as walking with your children is a great way to keep active and find out what's going on in their world.

15. That's Entertainment

If you want to see what children can do, you must stop giving them things.
Norman Douglas (writer, 1868–1952)

Entertaining my children when they were smaller was relatively straightforward. In the summer they would play for hours on a plastic fort that had built-in water sprinklers, and on colder days it was toys, TV and games. They played well together, mostly, and would invent games to keep themselves occupied. I have delightful photos of teddy bears waiting in line for a swing and slightly less delightful photos of them waiting nervously to play chicken with Hot Wheels cars.

As the children grew our games became more advanced and the three of us would battle to become champion of Monopoly, Cluedo or Hey That's My Fish. My brother, a board game aficionado, has kept us supplied with interesting European board games such as Zooloretto, Rat-A-Tat-Cat or Forbidden Island, which is one of the few board games you play as a team.

I also encouraged combining physical activity and games and in the summer months we can be found battling away at backyard cricket, volleyball, soccer or mini-tennis. These are fun and highly competitive – the odd tear has been known to appear. Unfortunately as your children grow you need to keep adding to the mountain of toys and games to keep them interested and engaged. So the opportunity to purchase some of the latest and greatest toys and games with a visit to Hamleys in Regent Street, London's oldest and largest toy shop, was a keenly anticipated stop during our holiday in England.

HAMLEYS

Hamleys was impressive: six floors jam-packed with toys and games. Liv, who had just turned nine, couldn't believe the ocean of teddy bears she was confronted with and she delightedly jumped from display to display. Rog, eleven, was interested in toys and models and we split our time between floors one and five. For once I was in no danger of losing them: they'd have to be chucked out of Hamleys.

The range of toys made selection difficult but eventually Rog and Liv settled on their choices. I counselled Liv that buying only teddy bears might not be a good idea and I gave her time to reconsider. She thought about this, or gave the appearance of thinking about this, but she decided to stick with the teddy bears she'd chosen.

My approach with the children in these situations is to offer advice highlighting what may happen but let them make the decision. The major exception to this is when it comes to sweets and chocolate. That's an area I patrol vigilantly, noting what is bought and when it's eaten. Logic and restraint abandon the majority of children when confronted with items radiating sugar.

With Hamleys ticked off the list, at least for two of us, we spent the rest of our time in London visiting many of the famous attractions. On our last day, a Friday, we were coming back up the Thames after visiting picturesque Greenwich. I was relaxing with a beer, Rog was taking in the sights and Liv was sitting next me quietly. Unless she's sick, Liv is seldom quiet. As we slipped back towards Westminster Pier she suddenly looked at me and said earnestly:

'Dad, I don't think I chose my toys very wisely.' She had clearly been mulling this over for some time because the sentence sounded more like my words than hers. I smiled sympathetically.

'Never mind, my little one. I did try to point that out.'

There was a pause while Liv considered this. 'Well, can we go back so I can buy some different toys?'

I had been contemplating a leisurely dinner and not a dash back to Hamleys via the Tube during Friday evening rush hour. 'Darling, it's 4.30 and London gets pretty busy around now. It will be a mission to get there.'

'We could try,' she said imploringly in the way daughters can but that you wish they couldn't.

When confronted with a question, or in this case an entreaty, from the children I ask myself – is this a battle I need to win? It's an insightful question that helps me determine if the issue is important or whether I can go with the flow. For example: 'Dad, can we have an ice cream' is a battle I probably don't need to win. If, however, it's the fifth time they've asked, then it's a battle I must win unless I want to be nagged into submission for the rest of my life.

This question works just as well when you're dealing with your significant other. If you heed the answer, you can save many potential stoushs over nothing. Needing to win is different from wanting to win, which is an easy trap to fall into.

I looked into Liv's hopeful eyes and decided this was a battle I didn't need to win. Who knew when, or if, we'd be back in London.

The London rush hour meant personal space on the Tube was at a premium. Liv hung on to me like a baby koala and stared up into my face for reassurance. Rog, who doesn't enjoy crowds at the best of times, wasn't rapt to be impersonating a sardine but he coped stoically.

We arrived at the well-named Oxford Circus to find rush hour had become 'get an effing move on' hour. Making progress, while not losing a child, presented a serious challenge. It's on occasions like these that having a partner and being able to split child-minding duties is a blessing. With a child in each hand we were a decent barrier to the on-coming human traffic which was flowing fast and in single file. In the crowd I found it tough to get my bearings and it was more by luck than good management that we weaved our way to Hamleys.

With a good deal of prodding, choices were made in record time. Liv chose toys and no teddy bears, though I laid down the law about that. Included were the magical-looking 'Lights from Anywhere', which Liv chose after watching a Hamleys employee make the lights disappear up his nose and come out his ear and other parts of his body. Rog was also delighted with more models and toys and we were soon heading back onto Regent Street. We were still three abreast but this time with shopping bag extensions.

I figured the worst was over and getting back to the Tube station was merely a question of retracing our steps. But I wasn't aware that some Tube entrances close at wildly inconvenient times. The closed gate in front of us gave us no choice but to dive back into the human current in search of another entrance.

Luck seemed on our side and we followed the crowd down a staircase towards the familiar Tube ticket barriers. As we approached the final hurdle, a guard started closing a metal gate door that looked eerily like those used on the *Titanic* to keep steerage passengers below. Resisting the urge to yell 'Give us a chance to live, you Limey bastards' we advanced – witnesses may have said charged – through the crowd as fast as was semi-decently possible. The guard, oblivious to the drama being played out around him, gave a final heave and slammed the gate shut – behind us.

'That was close, Dad,' the children said in unison.

THINGS

Finding ways to keep the children occupied has become more difficult as they approach their teenage years. When Rog turned thirteen he reached that awkward age between toys and adult pastimes. As a result he's become difficult to shop for on his birthday and Christmas.

He still has toys unopened from last Christmas. I came up with the idea of wrapping them up again but he was far from impressed. He told me that he was getting around to them. Yeah, right!

Liv, on the other hand, hasn't yet reached that awkward age and still adores the simplicity of teddy bears. She has an abundance of them at both houses. In fact, she has so many you would suspect that they've been breeding like Tribbles (Trekkies will know what I'm talking about). I'm loath to buy more and therefore she too is becoming difficult to shop for.

Even armed with the latest gadgets and devices, keeping children entertained remains an age-old problem. Blissful were the days when you could lie them on their backs with some plastic shapes to chew on while you sat, feet up, with a coffee. Now we live in an age where children have an abundance of the 'things' Norman Douglas describes – but are they happier or more productive?

On this subject I was fascinated to read an article by German philosopher Georg Simmel. He described how life in cities contains an endless stream of stimulations and distractions offered to us from all sides. We don't need to think anymore, he said. We merely swim from one distraction to the next. Simmel wrote that in 1903. That's before cinema, cars, radio, television, the internet, iPods and social media just to name a few of the things we now have. I shudder to think what he'd make of today's world and the time adults and children alike spend thinking.

It's a real tension for parents. How much do you let these 'things' occupy the children as you get through your day? In an ideal world I would spend the majority of my time interacting with Rog and Liv, but I don't live in an ideal world. Who's going to organise dinner, tidy up and do the washing – and that's after I've finished work to pay the bills. I might just want to put my feet up for half an hour and watch anything on TV to *avoid* having to think. Sorry Georg.

Whether we like it or not, technology has become a staple form of entertainment for children. While video games, as they were called in my day, have been around for decades, today's games are unrecognisable in terms of their reach and realism. Xbox, PlayStation and others allow children to play constantly and many, including Rog, would do so if they were allowed. There's no danger of running out of twenty cent coins anymore, though we wouldn't want our children visiting arcades unchaperoned in today's nervous world. Is the world *that* much more dangerous now? I used to walk to school from age five, but neither Rose or I for a second considered letting our own children walk at that age. That would be tantamount to a dereliction of basic parenting!

The increased realism of today's computer games has also been a dramatic change. The video games of my era were exactly that, games. You knew it was unlikely that invading aliens would appear in the sky in neat lines and start moving sideways dropping bombs. Today's games are scarily real and I wonder whether these games do have an effect on my children. Intuitively I think there has to be some effect, but research is unsure and comic books were once considered an avenue to delinquency. It may be a case of the more it changes, the more it stays the same. Only time will tell.

TECHNOLOGY

The other change technology has introduced, potentially more sinister, is the way it keeps children connected. That's a massive paradigm shift that I doubt we understand. Children used to be in contact with their friends at school, during after-school visits or by phone calls. In between, including school holidays, they were liberated. Now with the internet, email, interactive games, mobile phones and social media they're wired into the social grid during their waking hours. I can't know, but my suspicion is that future generations will wonder why we thought that this was a good idea.

I've tried most social media apps because I refuse to be one of those people with a strong opinion about something I've never tried. I caught my brother out recently when he told me the movie I was planning on seeing was 'average with poor acting'. I asked when he saw it and he hadn't! I have Facebook and Twitter accounts and I post and tweet periodically so I feel entitled to put forward my opinion that they're mainly time-wasting distractions. But I am in a minority, and the younger generations hammer them and other social media apps.

With technology dominating the environment I make sure my children get time away from screens and the rest of the world by having 'non-screen' time. Each school day between 6pm and 7.30pm, all gadgets and screens have to be put away, including mine. It gives us a chance to interact, make dinner together, play or just breathe. It takes the children out of the cyber world and brings them back into the real world. They usually start by slumping into the couches but within five minutes they've started reading, bouncing a ball, checking out forgotten homework or doing a jigsaw. I'm the same. If I turn off my laptop and phone then I'll drag them out for volleyball or a walk or I'll spontaneously start pruning a tree. It's easy to get slack when I get busy but I try to police it with vigour.

In the weekends the screens are kept at bay somewhat as the children, at least on Saturday mornings, are playing sport. On Saturday evening we often watch a DVD together and, while I appreciate the movie is on a screen, it's not interactive and requires your brain to engage with the plot. We set the lounge up cinema-like with the addition of blankets and pillows and fill the table with snack foods to munch on. When we watched *Castaway* I'd forgotten how emotional the scene is when Helen Hunt, whom I have a crush on, discovers Tom Hanks is still alive. After the movie had finished and I put the lights back on Liv said, sniggering, 'Daddy blubbed.'

Television remains a source of entertainment for my children but as they've grown it's been surpassed by social media and online content. This despite the number of channels having grown exponentially. Rog watches some sport, mainly cricket, and comedy while Liv gets hooked on hideous but addictive reality TV shows and cooking programmes.

Liv used to love the music channels and I wondered why she went off them, but after chatting to her it was obvious. The world has changed and the music channels have been left behind. Spotify, iTunes and other streaming services have changed the power balance, allowing listeners to play what they like, when they like, making music channels yesterday's news. If Liv wants to watch a music video then she can do so online.

One thing hasn't changed – music and growing up go hand in hand. Rog and Liv have entirely different tastes in music and keep me up to date with what's hot in their world. Liv is a top-twenty girl and listens to the latest hits, which are in my opinion, except for a few artists such as Pink, pretty awful. Rog on the other hand, taking after me, likes alternative music and plays Muse, The Killers or Skrillex when it's his turn in the car. Recently he put on 'Anarchy in the UK', which made me wonder how he'd heard of the Sex Pistols but I should have guessed, it was a game, Guitar Hero.

I've noticed that today's music (words that make me feel old) is far more risqué in image and language. Bump and grind has been taken far too literally with the clothes worn, leaving little to the imagination. Added to this is the frequency of swearing where only the 'C' word seems outlawed. It isn't only alternative or fringy artists either, number-one songs often contain a string of swear words. Why radio and TV stations bother to bleep out the offending words is beyond me. Everyone, children included, know what the words are. Pink's number-one hit 'Blow Me (One Last Kiss)' had the classic line 'Just when it can't get worse, I've had a shit day'. The radio station silenced the 'sh', leaving Pink having an 'it' day. That brings more attention to the word, not less. And shit, 'shit' is pretty mild.

It seems to me that society is still using 1900s thinking to handle swearing. We pretend it doesn't exist and bleep it out, maintaining the illusion of an upright – and uptight – society. My stance on swearing where my children are concerned is straightforward: they know which words are swear words so there's no excuse for using them. If they hear them in a song, or coming out of my mouth as they do sometimes, it's no big deal. I'll happily sing 'I've had a shit day' as we drive along – though interestingly I get told off by the children, who have weirdly assumed the role of language police.

While on the language theme, when the children got to that age when toilet humour is hilarious, I placed a ban on rude words. Having your children saying poo and fart in public is somewhat cringe worthy. To sidestep my ban my clever Rog came up with the concept of using 'edur' words. That's rude words backwards. Liv joined in with gusto and they invented words such as detraf, ttub and oop. I tried banning edur words too but it was a crafty mechanism and we all still use them today as a code when in public.

The times children spend hours without 'things' is probably rare, yet I think Norman Douglas is right. It's only when they're absent that your brain is fully engaged. In my own case, I never study or write unless I can block out a chunk of time enabling me to think and reflect at a deeper level. I'm considering extending our non-screen, non-connected time. I love the idea of spending time together in a hut without electricity, living basically. Maybe a good idea for a holiday although I can imagine the look on the children's faces, especially Liv, when I explain how a long drop works.

Reflections

- Setting times when no one is allowed to use screens is good for the children and family interaction.
- Technology provides entertainment but it is important to keep an eye on your children. Social media in particular can become very invasive.
- 'Is this a battle I need to win?' is a great question to ask yourself to help put issues into perspective. It works with children and significant others.

- Let your children keep you up to date musically – there's no excuse for being stuck in the nineties, eighties or worse.
- Don't get too hung-up about bad language – it's unavoidable. What is important is that your children know what is and isn't appropriate. And when!

16. School

Education has produced a vast population able to read but unable to distinguish what is worth reading.
George M Trevelyan (historian, 1876-1962)

You'll have gathered by now that my parenting style is best described as relaxed. Being a parent is much easier when you are having fun – in fact I can't think of anything that you do better when you're not having a good time. Being relaxed doesn't, or shouldn't, equal being slack and it's important that you get the details right, especially when it concerns school. I don't mind if my laidback style gets me into the occasional scrape, but I hate it when it affects my children. In particular it's been my tendency to leave organising school to the last minute that's bitten me on a regular basis.

Like all parents, I want my children to blend in at school. This is especially important on the first day of the school year when they are thrown together with a group of mainly strangers. I know we've all been through this process, and it may be good for a child's development, but my recollection of being lumped in with thirty random individuals was that it was daunting if not downright scary. Imagine this concept in a work environment – after the Christmas holidays you arrive at work and are confronted with all-new colleagues with eclectic traits such as: happy, committed, diligent, ambivalent, moaning, malingering and psychotic. No thank you. I prefer my existing happy, committed, diligent, ambivalent, moaning, malingering and psychotic colleagues. At least I know who's who.

Then there's the new teacher to navigate, who also has traits from the previous list. I don't want to further blacken my reputation with the teaching profession, but parents, students and children all know how enjoyable it is to have a first-rate teacher. It makes a world of difference. But it's a lottery. I was in love with my teacher when I was six and I got a pretty decent, and needless, smack in the head from another who was clearly in the wrong profession when I was eleven or twelve. I cross my fingers at the start of the school year and hope my children get someone who's at the top of their game.

THE FIRST DAY

In order to make school mornings easier, I purposely bought a house situated close to the schools that the children were likely to attend. This made the school run a stress-free stroll and has worked brilliantly. But it's the first day of the school year that's tripped me up on numerous occasions.

Rog's first day at his new intermediate school, a weird step in New Zealand between primary and secondary school, was also his first day in a school uniform. The week before school started – a whole week, mind – we visited the sole school uniform stockist to find that some of the required items were out of stock. I'm sure more experienced parents could have warned me about this, and it's obvious in hindsight that all the mid-range sizes would be in greater demand. I purchased most items but there were no school shirts. The very helpful shop assistant suggested that I try the second-hand uniform sale being held soon at the school. Mentally putting that in my diary, I ordered two new shirts which she was 'pretty confident' would be delivered before the start of the school year. Yeah, right.

Parenting lessons, the enduring ones, are mostly gained through harsh experience, and it turned out my next lesson was just around the corner. I learnt that second-hand uniform sales are not a gentle, retail experience and not for the polite. If you're serious about obtaining the items you need, you have to queue like a teenage girl after tickets to the latest boy band.

I arrived at the sale five minutes after it started, which to me was tantamount to early, to find it jam-packed. When I managed to jostle and squeeze my way into the room, I discovered the parental equivalent of a locust strike. For the second time in two days I was left staring at racks containing only XXS and XXL sizes. There are certain advantages to having a tiny or gigantic child. Megan, the children's first after-school carer, had a similar experience of the sale. She said she'd seen more order when a rare shipment of beer was delivered to their supermarket in Zimbabwe during the days of hyperinflation.

Leaving empty handed, I asked the security guard on the door how early people had arrived.

'About an hour or so.'

I started to leave but it suddenly struck me as unusual that a second-hand school uniform sale needed a security guard. I back tracked and asked the guard why he was here.

'Mate, I asked the same question. It's a school uniform sale, innit? But last time people barged in early and started grabbing stuff before they were open.'

I never stood a chance. I was competing with seasoned parents.

There were three days left before school started and I was getting desperate. Children, angels most of the time, can be vicious and merciless to anyone who stands slightly apart. *Lord of the Flies* isn't an extreme comparison. So acquiring a shirt for Rog became my mission. In my time as a single dad I hadn't cultivated a network of parent friends and that removed the option of borrowing a shirt. I knew, as a last resort, I could ask Rose to try her friends, but I was keen to avoid this, mainly due to pride. At that stage Rose and I were some time away from being chummy. My second-to-last resort was second-hand sales on TradeMe.

I'm no snob, but buying second-hand clothes isn't how I prefer to do things. Okay, I'm possibly a snob but I was also desperate. To my joy, it's funny how your perspective changes, a shirt was on sale that was near the right size. I contacted the seller and everything seemed perfect until he/she mentioned that the shirt was last year's style and that's why it was being sold. I learnt that the school had updated elements of the uniform for the New Year, including a new version of the shirt. WTF? I bet that really impressed parents who had children returning.

The new version of the shirt wasn't radically different to the old one (does anyone else sense a conspiracy between the school and the uniform manufacturer?). If Rog wore his jersey, even though it was summer, then I figured no one would notice. I purchased the shirt with a whole day to spare.

Having gone to all that effort, I wasn't terribly surprised when I was rung later in the day by the uniform store. The new shirts had indeed arrived. I wasn't annoyed. If I hadn't brought the second-hand shirt, the new shirts wouldn't have arrived. I know that logically the two events weren't related but, in Murphy's Law tradition, it seems to be the way the world works. There's another saying I use in my working life that I think is worth remembering – hope is not a strategy. I bought two new shirts and put the second-hand one away as a future last resort. It never saw the light of day.

With a large sigh of relief on my part, Rog attended his first day looking just like everyone else.

I walked Rog to school on his first day to make sure everything went well. I was astounded by the size of some of the children, who could have been no older than twelve but were Shrek-sized. While I found this slightly alarming, Rog was unfazed. When he found his mates he gave me 'the look'. Most parents of teenagers will recognise it, but this was my first time. It's an almost imperceptible flick of the head combined with a fleeting raising of the eyebrows. I took it to mean: thanks Dad, I do love you, but your presence is embarrassing so you can take off now. So I did.

Parental disorganisation take two was a mere day away when Liv started back at her school. I always try to treat Rog and Liv equally and this extends to sharing my incompetence. I had no uniform saga to battle with Liv and she went in her usual three-quarter jeans, T-shirt and jandals. We wandered in together in the warm morning sun, happy and carefree.

As we merged with the pedestrian tide I noticed the other children, along with their immaculately groomed mothers, were weighed down with bags full of stationery: exercise books, lined refill, folders, writing pads, art pads, pens and pencils. Liv, with her unshaven Dad in jeans and a T-shirt, was the only one empty handed (I fail to see the merit in dressing up for the school run but I wasn't single at the time). How had I missed this? This was not the way to start day one with a new teacher and classmates.

Whenever something goes awry there's a natural tendency to place the blame elsewhere. In this case I felt, wrongly, that the culprit was Rog's new school, which provided all the stationery he needed on day one and all I had to do was pay. Fantastic. All schools should do this, though I do understand the financial implications. Somehow I'd imagined that because it was so easy and made perfect sense, Liv's school must also be doing this. I had fallen into yet another trap for inexperienced parents.

Liv and I found her new classroom, which was crowded with children and parents and in a state of pandemonium. I picked my way through the melee until I reached the already hassled-looking teacher. Better you than me I thought – you've got a couple of hundred days to go before your next extended holiday. I explained the stationery situation to her. In other words I made up a plausible lie to cover-up my incompetence. I asked whether it was vital for Liv to have her stationery today. She paused ever so slightly before assuring me that it would be 'fine'. Fine is such a dodgy word.

I tracked down Liv and made sure she was happy, and explained to her that she'd be okay without her stationery today. She was bouncy as her new class contained a number of her friends from last year, that's always a bonus. She gave me my usual big hug and I went home planning to carry on my day – but the teacher's slight pause and use of the F word bugged me. I checked the stationery list, which I had placed prominently on the fridge to guarantee I wouldn't be in this position. It said, complacently, that the children would require the following items on their *first day* … About face. Quick march! I headed off, list in hand, to purchase all the required items.

Not everything was available, there's a surprise, but I managed to get most items and arrived back at the school thirty minutes later. I peeked through the window of Liv's class and saw the teacher holding up an exercise book and instructing the children how to label it. Not needed indeed. Every child was rummaging around looking for the right book except Liv, who was helping someone else. I stuck my head around the door, caught Liv's eye and held up the bag of stationery. She bolted across the room, startling the teacher who gave me her version of 'the look'. Unfortunately for her, and something many teachers forget, 'the look' doesn't work on adults. I was *so* tempted to give her a wink accompanied with a cheery 'Carry on, luv', but I didn't.

In the corridor a beaming Liv gave me a giant hug and grabbed the stationery.

'I told everyone that you'd gone out to get it,' she said smiling.
'But I hadn't.'
'But you did.'
'But you didn't *know* that. You lied,' I said smiling.
'I can't have, can I?' Liv held up the stationery to prove her point. Still beaming, she disappeared back into the classroom.

Sometimes it's the little things that make all the difference. If I'd believed the teacher would Liv have had a bad day? Might it have thrown her off stride for a couple of weeks? Probably not, but I'd already been scarred by a lesson in how Liv's schooling is affected by her happiness. When she swapped schools, in amongst the other changes brought on by the separation, she was exceedingly unhappy and wanted to return to her previous school and friends. In this frame of mind she scored 50 per cent in the entrance-level maths test. But Liv has always been a maths whizz. Six months later, an adjusted, happy and bouncy Liv scored 98 per cent in exactly the same test. My lack of organisation created the stationery situation, but I left knowing that Liv was happy. I left feeling like Super Dad.

MORNINGS

Once the children and I survive the first day of the school year mornings quickly become routine. Not routine in a monotonous way – routine in a structured way. I start my days before the children are awake with coffee and the news. I like to know what's happened in the world. I've done this ever since I received an email early one morning cancelling a meeting and cryptically remarking that he didn't fancy his upcoming flight. Puzzled, I turned on the TV and sat riveted for the next five hours watching the 9/11 coverage.

When the children were younger I would tip-toe around the house with the TV turned down to a whisper to avoid waking them. I wasn't concerned about waking them per se, but if I did wake them they would descend on me wanting breakfast in front of the cartoon network. In other words they'd force me to be a parent, and I wanted to stay an adult until at least seven.

Now they're teenagers and I can blunder around the house like an elephant because experience has taught me there's no danger of waking them. Rog in particular is difficult to rouse on school mornings, despite my singing 'Morning Has Broken' while whipping his curtains back to let the dazzling light consume him. Occasionally I have had to resort to beating him with his own stuffed toys – his

Wellington Zoo snake is perfect for this. Liv's easier to arouse. She staggers into the lounge and collapses on the sofa, leaving only her dishevelled hair sticking out from underneath the blankets she has dragged in with her.

Once coffee has worked its magic, I'm ready to face making breakfast and the school lunches. Breakfast is usually a plain affair but also sufficiently nutritious to get the children off on the right foot energy wise. I'm not sure why I still look on making school lunches as such a chore, as single-serve packs have made the process relatively simple. I don't care if I'm paying quadruple the price per volume: I adore the ability to stand at the pantry and throw packs of chips, biscuits, muesli bars, dried fruit or snack foods into lunch boxes. Add fresh fruit and a sandwich, which takes 90 per cent of time, and I can flee the kitchen.

I make a special effort to ensure the children's lunches are varied and interesting. This is because I snuck down to Rog's kindergarten and watched his face light up when he saw a mini-muffin covered with sprinkles. I love the idea of my children opening their lunch boxes and experiencing delight, and I've been trying to recreate that scene ever since. To do this I include treats, different snacks or obscure fruit like pomegranate seeds or banana passionfruit. It also earns attention and intrigue from their schoolmates, which is a bonus.

I dutifully check their lunch boxes in the evening to see what's uneaten. I'm mildly devastated when the sandwich is returned, usually unsampled. It's the one part of their lunch that has involved significant effort and I try to craft a delicious sandwich then sell it to them in the morning – today we have roast beef and homegrown lettuce on fresh wheat bread. Rog usually eats his; it's Liv whom I have to bully and threaten with reduction of other treats. I then have a decision to make about the returned sandwich – bin it or put it in the fridge for tomorrow. I reckon 90 per cent of mums would bin it and 90 per cent of dads would put it in the fridge, or eat it.

If it looks pristine, I give the sandwich, and Liv, a second chance. Never a third though. Honestly.

With the children fed and the lunches made, I quickly shower and just after eight we should be ready to go. When they were both at primary school we used to wander along together, the round trip taking about ten minutes. Now Rog is in high school he leaves first, as he walks with a friend, and I drop Liv about five minutes later on my way to work. Her school is closer than Rog's but she isn't a big fan of walking, especially by herself. I can understand that.

INJURY AND ILLNESS

School mornings run like clockwork – unless one of the children claims to be stricken with a virulent illness. Rog and Liv, and children in general, have no idea the chaos their illnesses cause. My day is planned, it has to be, and a significant part of it revolves around patting them on the head as they disappear off to school. 'You'll be fine' sums up my response to most of the children's illness claims. In order to have the day off school they have to be closer to death than they realise. I generally bang some paracetamol into their systems and say 'We'll see how you feel *after* school'.

Illnesses and accidents are an area where Rose and I see the world from opposite ends of the spectrum. Rog jokes that if he cuts his finger Mum sees a severed finger while Dad sees a scratch. I'll never forget the time I bounced Rog, five or six at the time, slightly too high on our trampoline, as dads do. He came down awkwardly, yelling out in pain and holding his back. It didn't look bad to me but I got him to lie still so I could give him an amateur once-over. Before I could start, the world seemed to slow as it does in the movies and I turned to see Rose bearing down on us in terminator style. If this was a movie, unless I was a superhero, I was dead.

Arriving at the scene in an instant, she took charge. I was genuinely impressed at her ability to simultaneously comfort Rog with tender words while giving me an absolute gob full. That's true multi-tasking. She then sprinted to the children's play fort, while cataloguing my shortcomings as a parent and adult. She had the intention of using the slide from the fort as a makeshift stretcher, but the fort wasn't intimidated and put up a brave struggle, momentarily deflecting her attention from me. By the time she had detached the slide and returned, Rog was back up and bouncing. I never said a word, but on the inside I smiled broadly.

I realise you're not meant to send children to school sick and I don't. But the recommendation to keep them home for a few extra days in case they're contagious – that advice can only have come from someone who is either childless or has a sock-darning partner. If the children are genuinely sick I don't send them to school, I'm not as gung-ho as I make out. One morning Rog, while not looking too bad, was moaning and lying lethargically on the couch. Sceptically I checked his temperature and nearly burnt my hand on his forehead. He was dosed up and packed back off to bed and I spent the day working from home.

It's a fine line judging illness from general malingering and, let's be honest, children like to malinger. We all do. This is especially the case if there's something on at school which is unpleasant, like a cross-country run. But slogging around a sodden, desolate, windswept, god-forsaken farm once a year is a right-of-passage and so I'm unsympathetic. It didn't make a man out of me but it did a good job on some of the girls.

As a parent you develop intuition about when something's really amiss with your children. It isn't anything in particular, but one look is sometimes enough to tell skiving from something serious.

One morning I received a call from the parent of one of Liv's friends. Liv, who was nine, had fallen off her ripstick and hurt her arm. Although the children weren't with me that week, and therefore I was off duty, I was thankfully around and I strolled down to check out my allegedly damaged little one. I could tell from the look on Liv's face that she was hurt and it was instantly obvious that

I needed to get her to the doctor. I pretended it wasn't too bad, and using her T-shirt as a makeshift sling we walked to the car while I kept up a dialogue to distract her. Ten minutes later, and with a decent dose of pain relief, she was being treated for a broken arm.

Signs at the doctor's asked patients not to use mobile phones, but I furtively texted Rose to let her know what had happened and that everything was under control. She tried to ring but, being the relatively law-abiding person I am, I had diverted it to voicemail. I texted back: 'I'll call when I can.' The phone rang again and she left a message. It was remarkably similar to the one I had heard during the trampoline incident. I deleted it.

Rose arrived about fifteen minutes later, calm and relaxed. It's amazing what a few deep breaths can do. Soon Liv was the proud owner of a fluorescent green cast and a story to tell the next day at school. She managed to look adorable in her cast and had been so brave throughout the ordeal. No tears.

POST-SCHOOL

I find after-school pick-ups aren't a problem, at least for me, and it's when having a reliable nanny pays dividends. Even when I'm nanny-less, picking up the children is painless. I know where they are and where they need to be and it's just a matter of logistics. Nevertheless, the number of extra-curricular activities such as sports, music and the odd detention has increased, and I believe I know what life would be like as a taxi driver.

One tactic that worked regarding logistics was to put all the children's pick-ups, appointments, events and practices in my own electronic work diary. I do this even for the weeks when they aren't with me because once when Rose and I swapped weeks I forget Rog's piano practice. It also taught me that relying on my son's memory is a recipe for disaster. Using my work diary in this way has given me a single place to check where we all are, where we need to be and what has to be organised and accomplished. The advantage of an electronic diary is that I can access it from both my laptop and my mobile phone.

Once the after-school activities are done and dusted, all that's left to do is empty and check lunchboxes, remove soiled clothing from their school bags, hang out togs and find out what homework they have to do. I used to police homework, but now they're older I've made it their own responsibility. I've drummed into them over the years that the consequences of not doing homework affect them, not me.

If I survive the first day of the school year and keep my children healthy, school days are stress-free. I've learnt many lessons the hard way but those are the ones that tend to stick. I envy those with the ability to learn from other people's mistakes. That's a talent I'd love to acquire.

Reflections

- Make school mornings as easy and as relaxed as possible. There's nothing worse than starting the day in a frenzy.
- Make sure you know what is required on day one of the school year so your children can blend in seamlessly.
- To avoid being left empty-handed when purchasing school uniforms, shop at least one week earlier than you judge to be ludicrous.
- Second-hand uniform sales are not for the faint-hearted. Go early and be prepared for battle.
- Single-serve food packs are a godsend for school lunches, despite the cost.
- Children like to malinger but they do also genuinely get sick. You need to become good at working out which is which.
- Putting all your children's appointments in your own diary makes it easier to coordinate your world.
- Hope is not, and never will be, a strategy.

17. The Ex

The opposite of love is not hate, it's indifference.
Eli Wiesel (professor, activist, Holocaust survivor and Nobel Laureate)

I suggest you avoid the vast number of blogs written by separated or divorced men and women. While they detail the challenges of life as a single parent they also usually incorporate their own brand of self-help and dubious advice. They're harmless but you often find not-so-subtle character assassinations of their exes. The following excerpt is from a blog rated in the top 25 by some internet mechanism for single-parenting.

> *While I was going through my horrifically Jerry Springeresque divorce I did what any shell-shocked new mom with an infant who had been dumped for the office floozie would do.*

She may have real grounds for portraying her ex as philandering, irresponsible and selfish. She has impressively achieved this in a single sentence. But what the writer is oblivious to is that writing in that manner reflects just as strongly on her own character, if not more so. It's completely one-sided. It's like a court case with the defence lawyer duct taped silent, so it reads as pure revenge. There are two sides to every story. When you only get one – and from an archetypal poison pen at that – the account becomes uncomfortable and difficult to engage with. I tell my children – usually when they're attempting to debate between themselves – that what you say reveals more about you than anything else.

Technology has opened up new avenues for individuals to tell their stories, but it's the speed from brain to the public domain that's the problem. Any form of writing is better for being read, critiqued and proofed. Not only is the writing vastly improved, you get feedback from the perspective of a reader and that aspect is extremely valuable. A book, as a finished product, is miles away from its first draft – this book is almost unrecognisable from the first draft I completed years ago.

The majority of blogs are closer to thinking out loud than they are to writing and I'm grateful my thoughts aren't broadcast unedited. This book has been subject to numerous, merciless edits from myself and others. You shouldn't throw the baby out with the bath water but sometimes the baby needs to be thrown out, sometimes all you need is the bath.

You won't find me subtly, or unsubtly, presenting my case as to why I was right and Rose was wrong in these pages. There is no right and wrong anyway. It's all subjective. This chapter is my perspective of how Rose and I went from day one to something like day 2500. How we went from being estranged to something closer to old friends though not exactly old friends.

THE COLD WAR

The early days were difficult as our marriage didn't end as a mutual parting of the ways; it ended like a volcano. Pressure over time slowly built to an explosion and explosions create damage. Thankfully, among the carnage that was raining down we both acted as adults. No one's clothes were destroyed, golf clubs vandalised (we both played golf), or anything like what's often associated with separations.

I vividly remember weighing up what to do about our joint bank accounts. Rose had the ability, as did I, to clean them out. Not that there was a lot of cash to hoover up – most of our financial empire was tied up in the house, but there was enough. I could have limited her access with a call to the bank, but I considered that would say that I didn't trust Rose to act responsibly. In my eyes that would have been as bad as actually hoovering up the cash myself and so I did nothing. As it turned out, it was the right thing to do.

Before the dust had settled Rose and I had to work out the best option for our children. In hindsight this is a textbook catch twenty-two. The very time we were least capable of communicating rationally about the children, we had to do precisely that. The children couldn't be parked for a few months or years while things settled down.

One of the major problems with the law, and how lawyers are forced to apply it, is that it treats everything as property. Bizarrely, the question becomes: who owns the children? Or, how are you going to divide them fairly? I can now see how far reaching those early decisions of ours were. We were effectively laying down a railway track, and once the track is laid then that's the way the train will go.

If your relationship breaks up and you don't have children then, as painful as it might be, after it's all done and dusted there's no reason to see each other again. Ever. There's certainly no excuse for drunken accusatory phone calls, emails and texts, though they're traditional.

When children are involved decisions about how care is organised are critical for them and for your future relationship with your ex. Our fifty-fifty shared-care arrangement meant we had to trust each other. Clothes, costs, logistics, schools, sports and a myriad of other issues and activities had to be discussed, agreed and coordinated. 'We'll discuss and we'll decide' is the way a fifty-fifty shared-care arrangement operates.

If one parent has the children the majority of the time then the majority of decisions should be made by that parent. In these situations the parent in charge can either employ a 'we'll discuss and I'll decide' policy or the more autocratic 'I'll decide', leaving the other parent to like it or lump it. I can't for the life of me fathom the logic of parents who don't want to do the parenting or caring but still want to call the shots. They tend to be male with a massively over-inflated view of their DNA's contribution.

Rose and I agreed on most things, but there were a few areas that proved more difficult, such as after-school care, extra-curricular activities and sports. It didn't take long to work out a range of compromises, which we put into practice to see what happened. At least I think that's what happened. It was likely tenser than that but, with the logistics settled, we got on with life.

The early part of the separation, which lasted roughly two years, were the eye-for-an-eye years. If either of us wanted, or needed, to change the arrangements then reciprocity was required, if not demanded. We hadn't planned to operate that way, but we both suffered from selective memory. Each thought the other was getting far more than he or she gave. So it became easier to horse trade at the time rather than accept a dodgy mental IOU. (By the way, it took quite a few edits to get this paragraph reading impartially!)

What Rose and I did brilliantly during the early years was take our conversations away from the children's eyes and ears. The disputes, debates and discussions were conducted via email, text or when the children were out of earshot. I said all but I meant the vast majority, we're only human.

One discussion that bubbled over concerned a proposed transport arrangement to which I didn't agree. Rose thought I was being obstructive and let me know this in no uncertain terms. It wasn't a major event but what I found disconcerting, and intriguing, was that both Rog (ten) and Liv (eight) sided with Rose, even though they had no idea what we were vigorously debating. I assumed their logic ran like this – Mum's upset and Dad appears to be the cause; therefore Dad is clearly in the wrong. Bad Dad! That was a lesson in keeping the children out of the line of fire.

During the first two years, apart from the first few months when tensions were understandably at their height, we were able to wander into each other's houses when we were dropping the children off. This made the exchanges relatively painless. Almost. It's fair to say our relationship was on the cool side of cordial but what was absent for all of us was the stress associated with apprehension. The exchanges fast became routine and not potential battle scenes.

GLASNOST

When Rose moved back to Palmerston North and we resumed the week-on/week-off arrangement then the remaining animosity, mistrust and hurt between us faded and disappeared. I'm not exactly sure what happened. It wasn't through a series of counselling sessions and most likely it wasn't any one thing. We didn't try and do anything differently but, on reflection, we'd been doing the right things all along and this created an environment that allowed it to happen when the time was right.

Ironically, we were sometimes called the ideal couple when we were together, which proved we were able to keep our private issues private. Now we were becoming the ideal separated couple – although judging by the stories I've heard there isn't much to beat.

If you're wondering what an ideal separation looks like in practice, well, on the surface there's little to notice. In fact our routines are similar to what many separated couples do, but it's in how we do them that the difference lies. Handovers are relaxed and we chat about what's coming up. If arrangements need to change it's now swings and roundabouts rather than an eye for an eye. I'm sure Rose owes me a few days but I'm also sure it'll equal out in time. More importantly, I don't care anymore. Maybe at one point she needed more time alone and I know for a while I needed more time with the children.

The environment we've created means we're able to do things that for many separated couples will sound impossible. Playing tennis doubles with the children or having family dinners – Rose even cooked once. We even went on a family holiday, just the four of us, as outlandish as that may sound. The major difficulty I had was finding hotels that catered for families without assuming the adults were going to share a bed!

In short, I think we've become like reunited members of opposing armies. At one point trying our utmost to kill each other and now able to share a drink and similar memories. At some point you just have to let it go.

What this doesn't mean is that we plan to emulate Richard Burton and Elizabeth Taylor and reconnect. I was taken aback when someone asked me why because Rose and I get on so well we didn't get back together. I guess it happens in some situations, but it just sounds wrong. In most cases like ours, the parents get back together functionally and logistically but not romantically. There's a chasm of difference between the two. It also doesn't mean that Rose and I don't annoy each other from time to time, although I'm pretty sure we don't annoy each other on purpose any more.

MISS CHIFF

An advantage of having a normal, adult relationship with your ex is that it makes it difficult for your children to play you off against each other. Don't be fooled by their innocent, angelic faces – they can be as cunning as foxes if they see a chink in the combined parental armour. My children's opportunities were severely limited when Rose and I started getting on better but they still nudged the boundaries wherever they could. Bedtime was a favourite.

'Mum lets us stay up until ten.'

'And?' I said.

'*And*,' Liv says with a calculated balance of attitude and defiance, 'we should be able to stay up *here* until ten.'

'That's right, Dad.' Nodding, Rog solemnly adds his two cents as though his considered opinion makes the decision obvious.

'Hmmm. I'll think about it and let you know.'

'When?' Rog asks with the same solemnity.

'Right after I discuss it with your mum.'

'*Why?*' It's Liv this time. They're tag teaming me and doing it pretty well.

'Why not? You're saying it should be the same in both homes so I'll compare notes with Mum.'

'Yes, but …'

'Yes, but nothing. Bedtime stays at nine until I've chatted with your mum.'

'Fine.' Liv uses the F word with a blend of impatience, annoyance and attitude. It doesn't work on me but I fear for her future beau.

'And by the way,' I add, 'if you're trying to put one over on me, I'm going to squish you both.'

Silence.

They had, but I didn't squish them – much.

I also discovered that Liv – Miss Chiff, as I call her in these situations – had been far more successful in her manipulation of entrées. Let me explain.

A popular restaurant we frequented both pre- and post-separation was the Lone Star. The restaurant served large meals, so I was reluctant to order entrées as the children then didn't finish their main courses, forcing (yes *forcing*) me to finish them. They – in hindsight mainly Liv with Rog's solemn silence taken as support – insisted that they *always* had entrées when Mum took them. Not wishing to appear as the meaner parent, I usually rolled over.

Leap forwards in time and we're at the Lone Star, all four of us, as a family for Liv's birthday. After we ordered our mains we were presented with the upsell: 'Would you like any entrées?' Liv sat up with wide expectant eyes and Rose ordered chips and dip and the Lone Star loaf which, from experience, is enough food to slow down a horse or two. Liv was beaming and I had the opportunity to remain quiet. Unfortunately, for Liv as it turned out, while I had the opportunity to remain quiet, I didn't have the ability.

'I don't order entrées, the children don't eat their mains,' I said trying not to sound too challenging.

'Yes we do,' the children cried in unison.

'No you don't,' I said and I noticed that Rose was staring at me in what I took for astonishment. An ex's stare isn't as scary as a partner's stare that contains the message that there's a price to pay for whatever transgression has occurred and you'll be paying for it later. Uri, my university colleague, tried the stare on me one day when we were working out who was going to send invites out for a shared lunch. Her stare was absolutely withering and I was impressed. But unfortunately for Uri all she got from me was laughter – and the advice that she keeps that look for her husband.

Even so, I was now wishing I had just let it go. But I had misread Rose's astonishment.

'I only order entrées because they say *you* always do,' said Rose.

'I order them because they, actually Liv,' I correct myself as the situation starts to dawn on both Rose and I, 'says *you* always do.'

Miss Chiff had been sprung, but she was smiling like the Cheshire Cat. She'd got away with it for years. Ratbag. You have to grudgingly admire when you get done over like a dinner – or in this case done over like an entrée – by your own children.

SUNSCREEN

With regard to your relationship with your ex, I think the wisdom Mary Schmich expressed in a column for the *Chicago Times* (which was made into a song by Baz Luhrman) can be adapted very well. She said: 'If I could offer you only one tip for the future, sunscreen would be it.' Her logic is that most advice is based on experience and opinion. Sunscreen, on the other hand, has been scientifically proven to be effective.

Using analogistic reasoning, if I could offer you only one tip for the future that will make your single-parent life easier, and make your children's life infinitely better, then getting on better with your ex would be it. I doubt there are scientific studies to support my claim but to me this is simply self-evident. But for it to happen, you have to make an effort.

This advice applies whether you're in a relationship or separated (just change the word ex for partner). It's in your children's best interest that you have a solid *adult* relationship with your partner or ex, and I think this seriously undermines the regularly cited theory that staying together for the sake of your children is preferable. It comes down to one of my favourite questions: what are you trying to achieve? Happy, secure, well-adjusted children who don't have to act as parents for their own parents is what I believe we are trying to achieve. If this is the case, then the question becomes a different one – what's the best way to achieve that, staying together or separating? If you stay together to simply last the distance or keep other people and deities happy and your children live in an environment that's less than ideal, I think you're missing the point. It's a marriage, not a sentence.

Having read numerous blogs and listened to stories from friends, I think many people forget a fundamental fact about relationships: two of the people involved in every separation are adults. If you're blaming your ex for your problems then you're acting like a child; you're part of the problem and not part of the solution. Adults sort out problems. Children name-call, slam doors, threaten, throw tantrums, storm off, don't speak to you and generally try to be as obnoxious as they can until they get their way. If your own behaviour has *any* of those elements then it's time to wake up and smell the coffee.

There will be cases where one parent is sadly misguided and deliberately uses his or her children as pawns for revenge or gain.

I've heard many stories of people using childish tactics such as stopping financial payments, not taking the children to events or to get their way by generally just being an overgrown bully. If your partner or ex is like that, I have to acknowledge that it makes life bloody difficult and you have my sympathy. When adults act like spoilt brats it's a tough situation to deal with. I hope I'm not being optimistic or naïve when I think that for the majority of people this isn't the case and each parent is trying to do what's best.

If you're in a situation where your ex puts their needs ahead of your children's and acts appallingly, I think you need to establish distinct boundaries. In this way you can *hopefully* control the frequency and nature of any interactions, thus minimising the impact on yourself and your children. For example, use school for changeovers. One parent drops the children at school in the morning and the other parent picks them up after school. I use the word 'hopefully' because you may need legal help to enforce the boundaries. Parents who don't 'get it' are unlikely to respect boundaries that don't have legal consequences if they're breached. The increased recognition of domestic violence, although long overdue, has been incredibly positive.

If you recognise your own behaviour is not in the best interests of your children, you need to quickly build a bridge and take responsibility for your actions. You may need help to do this and there are a range of options available that will help you work through your personal issues. There's *never* an excuse for acting like a child, even if they did do it first!

If you want an extremely positive example, Nelson Mandela spent twenty-seven years in prison and when he was released he bore his captors no animosity. How powerful is that! He exercised his *choice* to forgive and went on to do great things, incredible things. Imagine if he focused on revenge. His legacy, and that of the South African people, would be dramatically different and closer to that of Idi Amin or Muammar Gadaffi.

It's in your own best interests to choose to let things go. It takes considerable energy to keep bitterness and resentment burning and it's a waste. Do something positive with that energy and free yourself at the same time.

I don't intend to finish this chapter with my top ten tips for improving the relationship with your ex. I hope it's obvious that I don't believe that's the way the world works. If you want some tips use Google and you'll be greeted with thousands of results. In among the madness there'll be the odd piece of useful advice.

I think it's easiest to keep it simple. The things you need to concentrate on are the basics for dealing with anyone: trust, honesty, listening, keeping your word, saying sorry, being empathic, etc. My grandma taught me what she called the golden rule – do unto others as you would have them do unto you. It really isn't rocket science and as that advice comes from the *Bible*, it's been around for a while.

Ultimately it can all be summed up in the phrase 'act like an adult'. Being an adult has no correlation with age. It's about your level of maturity and there are many middle-aged children around. Calm, rational, fair, wise, self-sacrificing, patient, reliable, trustworthy and honest are words I associate with acting like an adult. No matter what your ex, spouse, partner, lover or good friend does, if you always act as an adult then over time your relationship with them will change. The logic behind this comes from transactional analysis – check it out if you feel like diving into the theory. Be wary though; academics and experts are great at making common-sense bloody complex and hard to understand.

And definitely use sunscreen.

Reflections

- What you say reveals more about you than anything else. Have a think about that before discussing your ex in a public forum.
- Keep your children out of all disputes, debates and discussions. They may be little but they have big ears and will form an opinion.
- If you're recently separated, or your about to separate, it's difficult to think and act fairly and justly but this is when you need to the most. Someone's got to take the lead, so it may as well be you.
- Separating is not an excuse for acting like a child, no matter who did what first. It's your choice whether you act like an adult or a child.
- Try to create an environment that allows bridge building between yourself and your ex, and those bridges will slowly build.
- If you get on well with your ex, your children will be less likely to get one over you. They will still try, though, and you may get taken for the odd entrée.

18. Travelling

I have found out that there ain't no surer way to find out whether you like people or hate them than to travel with them.
Mark Twain (writer, 1835–1910)

There are pluses and minuses to travelling with children when you're a single parent. On the minus side, a second pair of adult eyes is handy when you're trying to ensure no one is left behind or lost in the torrent of people encountered in airports and tourist attractions. Also, the comfort of being completely off duty when travelling is a luxury I haven't had in years. I've had to get used to reading with one eye on Rog and Liv and, when nature demands, going to the toilet in extreme haste. I remind my children, in my own fatherly way, that they too need to stay alert. It's become easier, but you have to stay alert as they're still children and I'm responsible.

On the plus side, I get to decide where we're going. That may not sound like a huge plus, but it removes any discussion about spending valuable holiday time visiting in-laws. That alone, I'm sure, would make it a massive plus for many people.

I choose destinations with Rog and Liv firmly in mind as you have to balance the perception of an idyllic family holiday with realism. Lounging around a pool all day, watching the comings and goings and waiting for the bar to open may sound idyllic. But paint into that picture two ratbags who've been asking 'What are we going to do now?' every five minutes and the imaginary joy evaporates. You also would have to pretend they aren't your children when they try and drown each other out of boredom.

Once I've selected our destination the art is to have fun getting there. I want to be the ideal travelling family where everyone, especially me, is having fun. More prevalent are families on the edge. The mother leads the way, determined and unblinking, dragging a small party of bored and rebellious children and the father plods five metres behind looking defeated. Next time you're travelling take a look around and you'll spot the stressed, manic parents holding it together because they're in public. That's no way to travel.

We don't have a part to play in those scenes. The children and I are in the smiling and laughing camp making the most of our travelling experience. It isn't luck having sensible and self-contained children, it's the result of consistent hard work. That effort is rewarded when we are journeying because they're like small adults and I can relax somewhat knowing that I'm unlikely to find one of them dangling over the rail of the ferry because the other laid down a dare. They aren't perfect, but a semi-loud 'Oi' is all that's needed to settle things down. That or I threaten them financially. Hitting them in the pocket always makes them think twice. Occasionally I have to play the big, bad dad, but that's because occasionally they're being little brats. Not often.

The trick is making travelling a part of the adventure and not a chore on the way to the adventure. It should be exactly the same for adults. If travelling is part of the holiday then there's no excuse for looking miserable. We actually live in a rather privileged age where travel is easy and available for many people (though not all by any means). Wind the clock back a few decades and most people stayed the majority of their lives close to where they were born. That's why the opportunity to travel, even if it meant heading to war, was so attractive to younger generations. That and the fact that war was criminally oversold as a fun adventure: two weeks in Europe or the desert and then home in time for tea.

The children and I have embarked on a range of holidays – both close to home and the odd major jaunt – and they've all been amazing and positive experiences. Experiences that I have no doubt will play a significant part in shaping their lives. When the opportunity arose to take the children to the UK it was a no-brainer. Yes it was expensive and no I'm not lucky. I used the bank's money. The only downside is that they want it back with interest. My logic has always been that one day I'll have the money to travel but not with the children, and so we need to travel now. I'll square the ledger in the future.

ENJOY THE JOURNEY

Leading up to the UK trip I sold the children on how much fun you can have on an aeroplane. I explained they would have their own screen and they could watch movies and play games. Even more attractive to Rog and Liv was the fact that we would get fed regularly. By the time we were packed and ready to go, although they knew it would be long trip, they were chomping at the bit. In case they got bored I was prepared with books, drawing equipment, magazines and snacks. My hard-earned lessons on parental organisation were standing me in good stead.

The first leg of the journey, which took ten hours, took us to Los Angeles and it turned out to be a doddle. The children happily watched movies and buzzed the flight attendants for extra snacks. Rog watched *Wallace and Gromit: The Curse of the Were-Rabbit* four times. Given there was a large range of movies to choose from, I found this … curious.

Liv was more eclectic in her choices and loved playing *Who Wants to Be a Millionaire?* As the questions are aimed at an adult audience, Liv drew me into her games and at each question she didn't know the answer to she would turn to me with hopeful eyes.

When my answers failed to deliver up a million dollars, as they did consistently, she frowned deeply. The questions were just like the TV game. They start at moronic – which fruit with a bend in it is yellow? They become general knowledge before you near the end when they become ridiculously difficult – if you planted the seeds of *Quercus robur*, what would grow? Although Liv was disappointed at not hitting the mythical jackpot, we all arrived in LA in great shape.

If you've travelled via the US then you'll be aware that in the post-9/11 world the Americans have developed an understandable, but unhealthy, suspicion of travellers. Even those from countries who are in the Five Eyes spy club with them. We weren't allowed to mix and mingle with other passengers and we were escorted to a secure transit lounge where the children discovered, much to their joy, that the snacks and drinks were free. My children are low maintenance and they tucked in with gusto while I decided that a beer was on the cards as it must be five o'clock somewhere. I then discovered there was no bar in this isolated part of the airport.

The two hours in the transit lounge went quickly in a blaze of chips, apples and sodas – but no beer. We were soon back in the air where tiredness finally overtook the children. Liv fell asleep on her tray table waiting for dinner and I'm not sure how Rog managed to curl up in his seat, but he did. I dozed off for a while but it's difficult to sleep for long and we were all awake again. Rog was back watching *Wallace and Gromit* (really?) and Liv, feeling miffed, was buzzing for snacks to make up for the dinner she missed.

We touched down at Heathrow airport twenty-eight hours after we'd locked the front door and the travel had gone without a hitch. More than that, it had been a fun, exciting experience and the right way to kick off three wonderful weeks together touring England and a bit of France.

But while an overseas trip maybe the ultimate travel adventure, you don't have to journey out of your own country to have wonderful family holidays. As many more New Zealanders have visited

Australia than Stewart Island, the smallest of New Zealand's main islands, I thought it would be a great trip for the three of us to tackle.

The children knew we were heading for Stewart Island but I didn't tell them how we were going to get there. They assumed we would be driving, but instead I developed an itinerary based on the film *Planes, Trains and Automobiles* that saw John Candy and Steve Martin have to navigate their way home using all manner of transport options after their plane was grounded due to snow.

'Who's in front first?' Liv asked as we locked the door behind us.

The front seat of the car has taken on monumental importance in my children's world because it means control of the music. When I'm feeling tired or hungover, and I can't be bothered refereeing, I announce 'Both in the back'. Liv's face will invariably appear at the front passenger window testing the water with a hopeful smile. 'Ten dollars' is my response – my charge if she insists on sitting in the front. Her smile will invert and she'll slink off to the back with a 'Poo you, Dad'.

'So, who's in front?' Liv asked again.

'Neither,' I said, smiling.

'Poo you, Dad.' She somehow managed to say it with affection.

'We aren't taking the car.' I enjoyed their confused looks for a moment before adding, 'We're walking.'

'Walking to Stewart Island, what the …'

'Now now,' I said, cutting them off unless they inadvertently completed the sentence.

'Walking to the bus station. Come on, we'll get breakfast on the way.' And we set off for Stewart Island on foot. I was wheeling our combined suitcase with the daypack over my shoulder. The children, ten and twelve, were carrying nothing. What a great dad!

The first leg of the journey was by bus to Wellington. I got the children the two front seats so they had a great view, something

I've always taken childlike pleasure from. We stayed overnight in Wellington and we were up early the next morning to catch the ferry, our next form of transport.

There's lots of time to kill when travelling, and to counter the boredom I was armed with books, magazines, iPods and a deck of cards. We found a comfortable spot near the café and I got out the cards. Liv, who adores games, sprang to life and Rog, just as keenly, put his book down.

'Last Card?' Liv said excitedly.

This was the only game my children knew at the time, apart from Snap and Pick Up 52 (which is only ever played once).

'No, I thought I'd teach you a new game, Euchre. We played it a lot in my cricket days when it rained,' I explained.

'Eureka,' Liv said, trying out the new word.

'Euchre. *You car.*' I annunciated it slowly to help get her head around the new word.

As Liv has grown she's given me many special linguistic moments. Recently she said to me, 'I know what you're up to, because I'm side kick.' Her sentence, as they sometimes do, stopped me in my tracks.

'Psychic?' I offered tentatively. Her face gave it away and, as I melted with laughter, I had to cover up as she rained down blows and admonishing cries.

Other memorable Liv'isms include a note with the words 'cereal killer'. I can't recall why she needed to use those particular words but it made sense at the time and I wasn't alarmed. Her use of the words 'tamofo' and 'o'sausages' had me smiling for days. If you're struggling to interpret them, I'll put them into the context in which she used them. 'Dad, do you use the font Tamofo?' And 'I've got a sore throat, I think I've hurt my o'sausages'.

We played a couple of open hands of Euchre so the children could pick up the basics and they were hooked. Euchre – although for Liv it remained eureka for most of the trip – became an integral part of our travels and our favourite evening relaxation.

Our next mode of transport was the Coastal Pacific train. I love trains, although not to the level of being a trainspotter, and the Coastal Pacific is one of the best train trips in New Zealand. Although we were one of the last to board the train, the lovely lady in the ticket office said she had perfect seats for us, and she wasn't lying. Three seats around a table right next to the observation car, an open car in which you can wander around and take in the view, and as far away from the buffet car and temptation as possible. Perfect.

We spent two days in Christchurch, where we saw at first hand the extent of the damage from the recent earthquakes. Parts of the city looked as if we had been transported to Aleppo or Beirut.

We hired a car to continue our journey, public transport south of Christchurch being problematic. We stopped at Dunedin, where we spent another two days taking in the sights. One place had the children bubbling with excitement – a tour of the Cadbury chocolate factory, where we ate and purchased enough chocolate to double our chances of type two diabetes. The Otago Museum and Baldwin Street, the steepest street in the Southern Hemisphere, were ticked off our list before it was time to be back on the road.

Invercargill was our last stop before Stewart Island. We stayed overnight and had an early-morning breakfast of muffins with hot chocolate for the children and coffee for me. Then we caught the bus to Bluff, the southernmost point of the South Island, where a catamaran was waiting to take us on the final leg of our journey across Foveaux Strait.

Nicknamed the 'roaring forties' for its latitude and roughness, it didn't disappoint. The swells were impressive and during parts of journey the catamaran more kangarooed than cut through the waves. When I thought it was getting particularly rough, I glanced at the captain, who was yawning. I took this to be a good sign. Rog's and my sea legs held up but Liv, who started out enthusiastically, ended up heaving over the back.

'I lost my hot chocolate and muffin,' she sadly lamented.

It took an hour for the catamaran to make the crossing and then, feeling like the intrepid adventurers we were, we stepped a little unsteadily onto Stewart Island. It had taken eight days but it was worth it from so many angles.

It's a familiar theme through this book that if you put in the hard yards you reap the rewards. Rose and I made travel fun – well, let's say *usually* as I have recollections of a few tense moments – and now the children are great travellers. That makes the absence of a second pair of adult eyes less of an issue. I love travelling with my children – they pass Mark Twain's test easily.

Reflections

- Plan your holidays with your children as they are and not how you would like them to be.
- Make travelling for your children a part of the holiday, a part of the adventure and not something to be endured.
- Children get bored when travelling, so think through what you can take to counter this. Simple fun, like cards, can be a great way to kill time.
- It doesn't matter where you take your children on holiday, it's how you holiday that makes it an adventure or not.
- Quercus robur is an English oak. That knowledge may help you win a million dollars one day, even if it's only to impress your children when flying.

19. Money

If you want to know what God thinks of money, just look at the people he gave it to.
Dorothy Parker (writer, 1893–1967)

Children are expensive and the costs escalate as they grow. The worst time seems to be the start of a new school year: the bills seem endless. There are clothes to buy as I discover how much my children have sprouted over the summer holidays. Rog, in particular, shows what the 1920s would have considered an obscene amount of ankle and his T-shirts have turned into muscle shirts. At least they would if he had muscles and so they're more rib shirts. Their shoes go from dainty and cute to clown-sized seemingly overnight and seem to last for shorter and shorter periods.

Then there are the school-related costs: activity fees, donations, camp fees and new stationery even though we now own more felts, coloured pencils and crayons than most preschools. Add extra-curricular activities such as cricket, tennis, piano and swimming, which all have fees and equipment costs and in Blackadder pelican style, no matter which way I look there's an enormous bill in front of me.

Apart from the costs children incur solely by their presence, there's also the list of things they *want*. It used to be toys and games, but now it's electronic game consoles, the latest phones and trendy clothes that are *needed* so they can blend in with their friends. It's not surprising children act the way they do considering how adults act. For grown-ups it's the same except it's cars, espresso machines, sandwich presses, golf clubs *and* the latest phones and trendy clothes. I like the sentiment expressed in *Fight Club* – we buy things we don't need, with money we don't have, to impress people we don't like.

Marketing firms have become stealthier than government spy agencies – although that doesn't appear much to beat – at targeting children and creating an ever-increasing demand for products. Companies have been taken to court for using a programme of planned obsolescence to ensure a constant demand for their products. I would love to write how I haven't succumbed to the rampant consumer world, and how my children only play outside in the healthy fresh air. But this book is based on reality and we aren't part of an Amish community. We've all developed a flair for spending money and it's usually the bank's money.

While I've developed a healthy aversion to accounting, I cannot escape its principles. The equation is simple: income is required to balance expenditure and I need to earn sufficient money to keep the children in the style to which they're accustomed. Although it's an unhealthy basis for staying in a relationship, I sorely miss being in the dual-income category – financially they were the good old days. In fact they were great. Rose and I probably wasted more money than we should have as your lifestyle tends to expand to hoover up any spare cash, but a dual-income situation has a snug feeling of security.

Coming back to my single-income reality, being self-employed has many advantages – flexibility, variety, control and, invaluable for a single dad, the ability to fit work around life. The major factor on the disadvantage side is the lack of certainty of income. My cashflow can best be described as irregular and I've learnt to ride the roller coaster not only financially but mentally. For over a decade and a half I've not had certainty of income outside a couple of months and becoming a SITCOM made me acutely aware of the delicateness of this situation. But consulting work usually materialises and, thankfully, this has been the case for me although it's not a comfortable situation. If you want a visual image of my situation, I liken it to being a tightrope walker without a safety net followed by a psychopathic, knife-wielding tax inspector. Disaster is waiting if I stop or fall.

JOINT COSTS

One of the complexities after a separation is working out how to contribute fairly to the children's costs. These costs are a joint responsibility, or they should be, and the quicker this is sorted out the better. Money, as evidenced throughout human history, has the capacity to be a dinosaur-sized bone of contention.

In theory, when you're a couple all costs associated with your children are a joint responsibility. My logic says that this situation should be mirrored if you separate. This will take different forms based on the working circumstances of both parents. Ideally this can be worked out fairly without the need for the authorities to become involved. In New Zealand the Inland Revenue Department decides on childcare payments if parents can't agree, though early in a separation this may present difficulties.

As a couple Rose and I put all our money into a joint account and that made sense when we were together. It didn't matter who earned the most, it was a principle. I would like to think that's what most couples do but it seems many couples run individual accounts with some way of ensuring that each contributes to the collective bills, including those associated with their children. This is a weird way to operate unless there is a legal requirement to do so. That's exactly what Rose and I do now because we're separated!

Isn't the point of being together – whether you're married, in a civil union or living in sin – is that you're in it together, including money? Separate accounts seem close to pre-nuptial agreements, which for me signal defeat before you've started. A friend's fiancé surprised her with a pre-nuptial agreement two weeks before her wedding. After deliberating for the next week, which included a lot of crying, she signed and went ahead with the marriage. She is, I'm pleased to report, very happy now that she's divorced. I have little time for anyone who uses their financial superiority as leverage over their partner; it's white-collar domestic violence and it's starting to be recognised as such in the courts.

To make things simple Rose and I agreed to replicate our married financial arrangement and split the children's costs fifty-fifty: school uniforms, fees, sports equipment, clothes, etc. Costs related to what you personally wanted to do with the children – for example when I took them to the UK – were your own. At the end of the month we send through a list of our respective costs and the required money is transferred by whoever is behind. We have upgraded this process and now use a shared Google sheet, very techie!

I need to stress that the reason why this works is that we *trust* each other to spend and claim money appropriately. If something crops up with a large dollar value then we discuss it first so that neither of us gets a nasty surprise when the costs come through.

Rose and I also maintained our practice of saving a small amount of money each fortnight in a jointly controlled account. We use this to smooth any lumps due to large expenses as well as creating a nest egg for the children's education. This has built nicely over the years and when one of our children had a recent medical issue we were able to use some of the money so neither of us suffered an abrupt cashflow issue. Again, this financial arrangement only works with trust.

Over time we've got shrewder from a financial perspective. At birthdays and Christmas we have stopped doubling up on presents, which is how we started and which the children loved for obvious reasons. We now jointly buy larger presents, like game consoles (if you can't beat them, join them) or mobile phones. I appreciate that this, and the other financial arrangements discussed, may seem remote for many separated couples, but Rose and I have been apart for over seven years. To me, it would say something about us as adults if we hadn't got to the point we are now.

MONEY AND TAXES

Keeping my books balanced while juggling the children-related money issues is one area but equally the children's own financial wants need to be managed. As Rog and Liv have grown they've become aware of money and what it can be used to obtain, like toys and chocolate. It must give the wrong impression to young children to watch you hand over a small piece of plastic which is given back to you with chocolate. It looks like a painless transaction and the sooner you educate them about what is involved in earning and spending money, the sooner discussions involving money become easier. Easier for you.

Rog and Liv were around eight or nine when I decided that it was time to introduce money more formally into their world by paying them for chores. I do recognise that I may be indoctrinating my children in the capitalist system, but that debate is for another forum. The concept I set up was simple and common. I linked money with genuine effort and so when they came to spend it, they had an appreciation of the effort it had taken them to accumulate it. It works perfectly.

They'll happily spend my money like water, which is understandable, but they've become far more careful how they spend their own. If we pop into a café for a weekend brunch, I'm happy to buy them hot chocolates. If they want a more expensive drink like a smoothie or a milkshake, then they have to make up the difference. It isn't the value that's significant – about two dollars – it's the lesson in actions and consequences. A huge bonus is that it changes the situation from pleading 'Please can I, Dad?' to the children quietly thinking 'Shall I or shan't I?' I find not being harangued in these situations is priceless. Rog usually chooses the hot chocolate and Liv the smoothie and both are happy.

The money-for-chores scheme also works well when it's time to pay the children on Sunday. The children know that the money they receive is based on what they've done, and consequently there are few arguments. Sometimes I can be a softy but I have to be careful not to undermine the whole point of the exercise.

The use of financial incentives and penalties does create interesting situations that resemble social experiments. I was washing the dishes, which meant the dishwasher was either full or broken, and I enlisted the children's help to dry them. There weren't that many but as they toiled away – their words not mine – the muttering increased about who was drying the most dishes. The situation came to a head with only the frying pan left. Rog and Liv both felt that they had unjustly borne the brunt of the drying and so each steadfastly insisted it was the other's duty to dry the frying pan. I watched and waited with researcher-like fascination for a resolution but a stubborn silence descended. In Dr Seuss fashion, the north-going and south-going Zax weren't budging.

'There's one thing you can bet on,' I said, breaking the silence. 'I'm not drying it.' And I was wrong. Both children instantly starting putting their case to me but, like a traffic cop on point duty, I stemmed the verbal traffic and ushered back the silence.

'I don't care,' I said slowly. 'You've both done half as far as I'm concerned. The question is, how you're going to resolve this?'

Silence.

'Here's an outrageous suggestion,' I said. 'How about a willing volunteer?'

The stubborn silence was replaced with an incredulous silence. I had to at least try what I hoped was the obvious solution. It was clear that each child had retreated to a fixed position and it was now a matter of principle and pride. It reminded me of when they were much smaller and I had found them, surrounded by an ocean of toys, arguing over the ownership of a piece of scrunched-up sticky tape.

'I could pay one of you to do it.' Liv's eyes lit up at this suggestion. 'But that would be wrong.' Her lights went out. 'Paying you to do something you should do for nothing sets a bad precedent. So here's the deal.'

The children remained stoic and I didn't get the usual groans that accompanied my deals.

'If I dry it, I'm going to charge you two dollars each. You can consider it Daddy tax.'

I hoped that one of them would realise the stupidity of their position and dry the pan, thus giving him or her the moral high ground in future disputes, at the very least. Neither moved.

'Alright. Five dollars. Each.'

The more-than-doubled tax had no effect.

'Let me get this straight. You're both going to lose five dollars because neither of you is prepared to do a job that will take less than ten seconds?'

In the ensuing silence I felt my annoyance move towards anger, but I was wasn't sure at what. Was it my inability to resolve the situation – or my children's pig-headedness at something inconsequential? In my work interactions, and the majority of my personal ones, I try to be the calmest person in the room and so, with a long soothing breath, I let it go. I resorted to the dreaded F word.

'Fine.' At least I kept my eyes open.

I dried the pan slowly, making the task take three times longer than needed, and then I put it away with exaggerated care. The children were still standing in the kitchen, though now looking sheepish.

'Can I help you?' I said cynically.

'Dessert?' Liv said tentatively.

My look gave Liv her answer, although inside I smiled at her cheek. They trooped out of the kitchen, wisely without argument. I hoped they had learned a valuable lesson though I doubted it. I've learnt and relearnt lessons throughout my life, which means I never learnt them in the first place.

I include the children in decisions with a financial impact that directly affects them for two reasons. First, it teaches them that there are both costs and consequences to the things we do and that means we sometimes have to compromise or make trade-offs. Second, and probably more significantly, they are part of the decision and get to understand *why* it's been made.

When we exceeded our internet data limit (which by the time you read this I hope is a historical notion) and suffered the cruelly named penalty of being throttled back, I had a decision to make. I say 'we went over', but it was when I had the children for two weeks in the summer holidays and the interactive games they play suck data like a runaway vacuum cleaner on maximum. Rog and Liv knew something was wrong long before I received the cheerful email informing me they had us by the throat.

'What butts is this?' Rog's attractive new saying for expressing displeasure.

'What butts is what?' If you can't beat them, or beat it out of them, join them.

'The internet is taking forever.'

'It's probably a glitch, give it a minute or two.'

Much less than a minute or two later.

'It's still butts.'

'My computer is really slow too,' Liv said, taking out her earphones and joining the conversation.

'Okay, don't get out of your prams. Let me check.'

I went to an internet speed-check site and started the test. The needle on the dial, which looks like a car's rev counter and usually soars magnificently near the danger zone, hardly managed to lever itself off the bottom; we were literally crawling. It was then that the news was confirmed via email that I paraphrased for the children.

'Dear valued customer. Blah, blah, blah. You're out of data and we are choking you until the end of month because we can.'

'End of the month!' they exclaimed in unison.

'End of our monthly cycle which, according to them, makes it until Monday. Four days.'

WTF, OMG, poo them and many other colourful phrases ensued before a thoughtful silence descended. I thought they had gone back to their games, slow as they were, but Rog had been thinking.

'You can buy more data, Dad.'

'Can I?' I said slowly with emphasis on the 'I'.

After some painfully slow searching online I learnt that my only option was to double our data for $30. It took us twenty-six days to use our 80 gigabit allowance and now I had to buy another 80 for four days, the majority of which would be wasted. I was outraged. If I could buy eight gigabits for $5, more than double the price per unit, I would have done it in a heartbeat, but this was a rort. It isn't as if our delightful customer-focused internet provider has to do anything as it's all automated. How to keep your customers 101: don't bend them over the table just because you can.

I explained the situation to the children who looked both thoughtful and hopeful but stayed quiet. I had an idea.

'Okay, here's the deal.'

This time I got groans and rolling eyes.

'I think that $30 for four days is completely over the top. As you two are the ones who really want the speed, I'm willing to split the costs three ways, $10 each. Otherwise we suffer.'

'In silence,' I added.

There were the usual questions, angling, protests and negotiations. When the dust settled, neither wanted to pay and so we surfed for the next four days at dial-up speed. There were no further complaints about the speed, though I was asked numerous times about the exact moment in time when we would be let loose again at warp speed. Although the house was limited to dial-up speed, I discreetly used my mobile phone's personal hot spot feature when I needed speed. You do have to keep a step ahead of the rabble.

The best things in life may be free but we live in a society where little is given away. So, irrespective of your political leanings, you and your children need money. It may well be the root of all evil, but it's usually the lack of money that causes the problems. Being a single parent has many challenges and money is certainly one of them, but the day you sort out equitable arrangements with your ex and educate your children about money is the day you remove a layer of stress from your life.

Reflections

- Children's costs grow as they do and they're unavoidable.
- It doesn't matter whether you're separated or a couple, your children's costs are a joint responsibility. Using your financial position as leverage is a tactic for bullies and cowards.
- The sooner you sort out equitable financial arrangements with your ex, the sooner life gets easier. Treat them as you would like to be treated.
- Trust is the key element when organising financial arrangements. You have to both trust and be trustworthy.
- Introducing children to how money operates is necessary. Getting them to be part of the decision making also helps their understanding and cuts down on their moaning and groaning.

20. Friends

If you have two friends in your lifetime, you're lucky.
If you have one good friend, you're more than lucky.
Susan Hinton (writer)

I think Susan's right and that's because there's a big difference between friends and acquaintances. The majority of people I know, those who float in and out of my life, are acquaintances. They're people who are fun to be with, most of the time, but who aren't friends in the sense referred to by Susan. The term 'friend' for her implies a relationship of considerable depth.

The concept of friends has been hijacked by social media, most notably Facebook, and they have used the term in a way that's meaningless. Friends for Facebook is a numbers game, a way of keeping score. It 'likes' – another hijacked concept – to keep you informed as to how many or how few you have. I better declare up front that I'm not a fan of Facebook. I use it to keep a wary eye on my children, to promote this book – which is hypocritical, I know – and to make sure I know how it works from personal experience so I can make up my own mind about its usefulness. When I last looked I had eighty-four friends, which is apparently modest. Well I don't. Using Susan's definition, on Facebook I have zero friends, some acquaintances and the rest I wouldn't recognise if I tripped over them. I literally haven't seen them in decades.

If you share your news about your separation on social media by something as questionable as changing your relationship status, it will be just another chirp in the newsfeed of your social media acquaintances. Most will miss it and it will be quickly usurped by the regular addition of recipes, selfies and recycled, repeated, unoriginal advice. Real friends are there with you, they know what's going on when someone gets caught up in the ripples of a separation. Separating doesn't just cause a split in your immediate family – it causes a split in the social fabric that surrounds your family.

From my experience there are two types of friend who emerge when a separation occurs. The first are those who are ready and available to help if needed but just as ready to give you space if required. They provide support for both sides without bias. When the dust settles these friendships have a good chance of enduring.

The other type takes sides and I believe these friendships are doomed. Obviously the side abandoned will want little to do with them but even the friendship with the side that they've chosen is likely to be uncomfortable. Taking sides simply isn't an adult action unless something objectionable has occurred such as the separation was caused by you sleeping with their spouse.

The great news is you find out quickly who's who. When I rang one mutual friend to find out what time we were teeing off in a golf tournament, he informed me that given the separation he wanted someone else in his team. I can't *know* what he was thinking, but I suspect he was under instructions from his wife who had strongly taken sides. One thing is for sure, you can't change what people want to think but it gives you a clear insight into who they are. I haven't spoken to him since I put the phone down. In the case of my separation the vast majority of our friends were, thankfully, of the unbiased variety, and that begs the question: why have I managed to end up with so few of them?

A SMALL CIRCLE

This lack of friends was highlighted to me when Rog and Liv's passports were due for renewal. Their applications had to be endorsed by someone other than a family member, who had a valid New Zealand passport and had known my children for at least a year. That isn't onerous but I struggled to come up with many options. Most of my student colleagues were from overseas and in my working life, as a consultant, you don't socialise closely with clients. Consequently most people who I could term work colleagues had never met my children. I did finally find an ex-colleague who met all the criteria who happily helped, but it was the fact I didn't have dozens of options that alerted me to my small circle of friends. It was more a ring than a circle.

My curiosity piqued, I did a stocktake of who had actually visited my house since I separated. Once I removed Cathy, my nannies and family members from the list it was sadly revealing. It was a fifty-fifty split between friends and tradespeople. The most frequent visitor was Eddie, the meter reader who I used to play cricket with. Stab your finger on the page and you'd as likely pick out the plumber as you would a couple over for a barbeque. The list was a little embarrassing, a bit sad and rather funny.

More concerning was that Rog and Liv were equally quiet on this front. I could only recall three or four times when they'd had friends over during the past seven years. It wasn't because each time the experience was terrible. On the contrary, I went out of my way to make sure time, space, activities and food were arranged. I may add that I even baked once. The visits all went off brilliantly. But their scarcity is because the majority of the children's social events occur at Rose's house – and I'll get to why I believe that's the case shortly.

The absence of visitors also doesn't mean that I'm friendless, although the majority are closer to acquaintances. I meet them down the pub on a Friday or for a coffee during the week but that's often the limit to those relationships. The chance of one of them popping over unannounced is remote, in fact I can't remember it happening. This can be a good thing as it means you don't have to worry about being caught 'a little worse for wear' by an unexpected guest. On the flip side, it means there's no reason not to get 'a little worse for wear' on a Friday or Saturday night. When I haven't got the children, of course. I do have a couple of close friends whom I've known for years but we can go quite a while between visits. It's a male thing.

Reflecting on how I became like this – and I can't speak on behalf of all single dads – I do feel that I might be typical. There are a few factors in play. First, and I know I'm generalising, females tend to be more outgoing and males prefer to be more insular. The majority of friends Rose and I had developed as a couple started as female friends of Rose and I subsequently developed a friendship with their male partners. After we separated, with little in common, these friendships quietly died a natural death. Like plants without water.

The friendships I've personally developed through sport or work exist mainly within those settings. I still see many of these people today, and it's always a friendly and warm exchange, but that's it. Either of us may say 'We must catch up', but in the male world we count the time in years rather than weeks or months.

That explains in part why my pre-separation circle of friends hasn't been replenished by a swag of new friends. The other factor not helping was my long-distance relationship. It's simply easier to socialise as a couple. A single, female friend lamented to me that it was 'soooo' much more relaxing going to dinner parties as a couple than alone. Due to this factor, by finding a convenient excuse I tend to decline more invitations than I accept, which means the invitations dry up. The answer is not as simple as pairing up with someone in the same boat because not wanting to be alone is hardly a good basis on which to found a relationship. It would, however, be nifty to pair up in a platonic fashion, though I imagine relationships of that nature would likely be fraught with the obvious complications.

LABELS

A more disheartening reason why I think the invitations become scarce involves image and insecurity. Society has a habit of labelling and stereotyping groups of people. Politicians, athletes, cougars, Asians, disabled people, single mums, terrorists, bureaucrats, the unemployed, etc. These labels are heavily associated with images, emotions and prejudices.

Without doing the research I'm uncertain how society views those of us under the label 'single dad'. I'm confident that we aren't seen as heroic martyrs, sacrificing fame and fortune to ensure our children get the best start in life. I feel we're probably closer to the absent dads I described previously: distant from our children who are being raised by their mothers while we injudiciously cavort our way through life. It's this view that I think creates unease in our erstwhile peers – hitched males who view us as potential foxes best kept well away from the chicken coop. In effect, I went from being a family man looked on as a fine, upstanding member of the community to a questionable individual, most likely an irresponsible and missing-in-action dad. It's quite a reputational fall from grace considering it's still me.

Whether or not they're accurate, labels and perceptions are powerful and trump logic and commonsense. I experienced a similar situation when I was made redundant. When it became known that I was for the chop, my interactions with colleagues changed. There was a stigma attached to me as though I'd been found discredited or dishonourable. A colleague and fellow casualty noticed it too and said he felt as if he had a communicable disease. Everyone was thinking it prudent to avoid being near his corporate corpse.

It didn't help that I was required to work out my last month but had literally nothing to do as my work had been reassigned. This left me in an office desperately wanting to appear busy and vital but figuratively with my feet on the desk. To lessen the tension I thought it best that I enjoy my last month gadding about in the company car before it was reclaimed. What did they expect me to do?

My first experience with the single-dad label was when Sam, my soon-to-be nanny, informed her mum that she'd been offered a job nannying for a single dad. Sam didn't see this as an issue and was keen for the job, but her mum had concerns and wanted me checked out. So Sam visited with her dad and we all had a nice chat. I didn't mind, as I had nothing to hide, and I clearly passed the character check. Sam happily nannied for me for years.

I'm not the only single dad to have had these experiences. A colleague related a story to me about when he was in Wellington in the 1980s and was a sole-charge single dad to three children under five. Circumstances saw him go from a high-flying businessman in the city to a stay-at-home dad almost overnight. Initially he was invited to morning teas and lunches by friends who were mainly married women with children. However, the invitations slowed and then abruptly stopped. The reason, he discovered, was that as a single dad, and despite being in a similar situation to his female counterparts, he was seen in the 1980s as being likely to display morally questionable behaviour. Disapproving husbands made it clear that having a single dad visiting when the man of the house was absent was the beginnings of a social scandal and couldn't continue. In his words it made for eight lonely years until he met his future wife and returned to his career. Only then did he stop terrorising suburban Wellington. It would be nice to believe that thirty years later we live in more enlightened times, but I'm dubious.

A more general factor is the perception that when it comes to looking after children dads are hopeless. I'm sure parents are more comfortable when their children visit with nuclear families or single-mum homes rather than with single dads. Cathy agreed and said she'd be considerably more apprehensive if her children attended an event, such as a sleepover, with a single dad in charge.

Even though I have a major problem with the logic, as there's a suggestion of something sinister, I'm more than happy to use it to my advantage to cheerfully avoid hosting children's events such as parties and sleepovers. Looking after multiple children of any age overnight isn't high on my bucket list, in fact, it's below appearing on a reality TV programme. Consequently, parties and sleepovers occur at Rose's house, where I can pop in and enjoy the evening's festivities but miss the aftermath, including the lack of sleep and cleaning up.

I naturally don't share this concern about single dads. Liv once went to a sleepover and birthday party where Pete, a recent single dad whom I had known for years, was the host. Did I see him suddenly in a different light because he had separated? Absolutely not. I did think he was mad having a sleepover. He was probably nagged into submission by an ex-wife/daughter combination, which can be lethal.

I am aware that as the children grow and become more self-assured my single-dad 'Get out of jail free' card will become invalid and I will be the welcoming host to teenage parties. My plan is to seek advice from some hardened campaigners. Hopefully everyone will have a good time, no one will get drunk and nothing will be spilled on the carpet. I can live in hope.

My final word, maybe it's a plea, is that when you hear the term 'single dad' think 'hardworking, dedicated *family* man who loves his children'. Just like you do when you hear the term 'dad'. In fact, just ignore the word single. You can invite us over without fear. We have been separated only from our former wives, not from our morals.

Reflections

- Real friends are few and far between and are unlikely to be found among social media acquaintances.
- One benefit of separating is that it allows you to determine which friends are worth keeping.
- It's easy as a single dad to become isolated and end up with a relatively small circle of friends. This is not necessarily a bad thing, it's simply the way it is for now.
- Socialising as a single amongst couples is taxing. Try developing a platonic friendship so you can change this dynamic and let me know if it works out.
- Single dads may not be viewed very highly in our society and that's wrong. In the meantime though, feel free to use it to your advantage to avoid hosting sleepovers and parties.
- The only difference between a single dad and a dad is the word 'single'.

21. Dating

In its purest form, dating is auditioning for mating and auditioning means we may or may not get the part.
Joy Browne (psychologist)

Long-distance relationships are tough, full stop. Even living in a world shrunk by technology allowing Cathy and I to keep in touch for free 24/7, it's not the same as being together. Video calls allow a level of intimacy unheard of a decade ago, but while this helps I believe it merely buys you time. We maintained the closest relationship possible, given the 19,000-odd kilometres between New Zealand and England, for over four years before our time ran out. Logistics became difficult, if not impossible, and it all culminated in a sudden, unexpected and terminal end.

That's enough about that. In the same way that this book isn't about my separation, it equally isn't about the demise of my relationship with Cathy. Given the time, effort, distance, joys and mistakes, I feel eminently qualified to write about long-distance relationships, but that's for another time and place. I went in with my optimistic eyes open but sadly for all romantics, which includes me, sometimes love isn't enough. Maybe it's never enough.

The demise of my relationship meant that for the first time in twenty years I was single. As I explained earlier, my relationship with

Cathy had shielded me from the trials and tribulations of the dating scene which now beckoned. My plan B wasn't to become a monk.

I didn't rush headlong into it and I took some time out to reflect and regroup. I spent the time working, studying, looking after my children, writing and drinking. It's a popular view that writing and drinking go hand in hand, with writers commonly portrayed as being at their best when inebriated. But except in a few cases I doubt it's true. If you think you're more likely to write fluently and from the heart when under the influence, you'll usually discover in the light of the next day that your output is closer to drivel than literature. So, incidentally, will be your emails, texts and blogs. Putting any writing into the public domain when you're the worse for wear is simply a bad idea.

IN THE MARKET

What eventually rekindled my interest in dating was being approached by a work colleague. I'd had a meeting with, let's call her Jennifer, on Friday morning and she sent a text through later that night to see 'how I was'. I thought – hello. We swapped a few texts and the result was we agreed to meet up for a date. It was a bit of a shock, albeit an exciting one, and it forced me to take stock of myself as a date and all that might entail.

On the positive side, although I'd turned forty-seven, which sounds old, I've always looked young for my age. When I was twenty I struggled to look fifteen which, unhelpful at the time, was something I was thankful for now. Also, given I'd been asked out, I must still have a measure of the 'Cor, I'd do him' look thanks to karate and the regular gym sessions.

Through the accident that's genetics, I still had my hair, which was another plus. I may have been the last to shave amongst my school friends, but some of their hairlines had been receding before they'd left school. Nature can be very cruel like that. I was also fortunate that the colour of my hair, mousey blonde, masked the grey well. Even then, current fashion dictates that grey hair on men is distinguished thanks to celebrities such as George Clooney, so I wasn't under societal pressure to dye my hair. Finally – and I know it's hard to judge your own personality – I don't have trouble making conversation and friends though I'm closer to shy than outgoing. All in all, as a package, I figured I had a few things in my favour.

I was, of course, a single dad and this meant that I was a package deal for anyone interested in anything longer than a few dates. I didn't see this as a negative as most men my age would have children. Besides, I was a much nicer person for being a dad, single dad, father and parent. I subsequently discovered that single dads are held in relatively high regard by single mums, who are acutely aware of the effort that goes into being a successful and happy single parent.

The only issue I saw with my children was the need for secrecy. I intended my dating to be something they knew nothing about. They'd met Cathy but, her visits apart, we were the three musketeers and that was how it was going to stay. Unless of course Miss, Ms, but hopefully not Mrs, Absolutely Right turned up. One can, and should, live in hope.

Before my first date in two decades I was, as you might imagine, nervous. I dressed in jeans and a casual shirt with the sleeves slightly rolled up to give what I hoped was the appearance of unfussed nonchalance. When I picked up Jennifer she looked stunning but casual and so, thankfully, we were on an even footing dress-sense wise. She'd also gained considerable height thanks to her high heels and was able to look me squarely in the eye.

I'm sure many first dates don't go well but, surprisingly, this one went exceedingly well and we ended up chatting into the night sitting under the stars. She seemed lovely and this dating lark was off to a promising start. It was, therefore, disappointing that our next, and as it turned out final, date turned out to be a bit of a nightmare, for me at least. I left her friend's fortieth birthday party at a local bar, in hindsight a bad choice for a date, early and alone. I had drunk too much and had been forced to make small talk with the other males for what felt like the entire weekend before politely letting her know that I was ready to go though I was more than happy for her to stay. The night left me a little worse for wear and feeling unsociable.

Despite the second date, Jennifer and I kept in touch but it was clear we weren't right for each other. We had, for example, polar opposite views on the subject of sex before marriage, which was going to be a source of frustration for one of us.

Those two dates got me back on the horse, figuratively, and interested in female company. The issue I now faced, an issue that I'm sure confronts most single people looking to date, was meeting new people. It's a lot harder than you may think. The number of new individuals who entered my rather limited social circles was somewhere between zero and low. I mean, how often do available people actually wander into your orbit? Even if they do, you have to fancy them. It isn't, or shouldn't be, a case of anyone will do. Traditionally, to meet new people you need to either start mixing in new circles or become a bar-fly.

With my consulting, study, writing and being a dad, I didn't have the time or inclination to take up a new pastime such as bridge or dancing where the primary purpose was meeting new women. As for picking up women in bars – I should say more accurately *trying* to pick up women in bars – it's a fun way to spend an evening ... when you're twenty. When you're closer to fifty, much closer, it oozes of desperation. Then there's the small question of who you may meet in a bar. If you sense you have spied Miss Could-Be-Right through the gloom and strobe lights at some ungodly hour, then it's definitely time to go home. Alone.

It's a long time since I viewed a bar as a place where I would meet someone stimulating. Bars are colloquially referred to as 'meat markets' for good reasons. Bar-room etiquette also requires the confidence to approach a woman and start chatting. 'Do you come here often?' or 'I haven't seen you here before' are standard lines and rather grim. As for anyone who uses lines like 'Remember me? Oh, that's right, I've only met you in my dreams' – he deserves to be cleaning vomit off his shoes for a fortnight.

Given the difficulty associated with that initial contact, it's no wonder that successful males in bars resemble, in looks and personality, stereotypical real estate agents, sales reps or used car salesmen. Cocky, mouthy and used to handling rejection without batting an eyelid. In keeping with those industries it's a numbers game in which persistence is rewarded.

But I should be careful about becoming over-judgemental or moralistic as I realise it doesn't take much alcohol to become one of those men I have just described (although I'd like to think I'm up a notch or two). But, as one of my favourite jokes suggests, the difference may be slight. We'd all like to believe that we're part of the modern generation of males and are SNAGs (Sensitive New Age Guys) rather than CHOPs (Chauvinistic Homophobic Old Pricks).

But what does it take to turn a SNAG into a CHOP? The answer: usually about three drinks.

ONLINE

Like them or hate them, bars are at least one of the few places where it's possible to meet new people. This situation has been radically altered recently with the emergence of the internet and social media which in turn have led to an explosion of online dating sites. The reason these sites have been so successful is that we can engage without the stress and tension of doing it face-to-face. Internet dating has replaced the need to put on your finery and hang out in bars, which is probably not a bad thing.

Until recently meeting online used to have negative connotations and was associated with gullible people being separated from their money or becoming unwitting drug mules. This has changed and online dating sites have become mainstream, a topic able to be discussed in polite conversation and on TV. The dating sites, at least the reputable ones, have become a good way of finding available people. Rather than embarking on a blind date, you get to read something close to a CV. Vitally, unless you are crazy and like taking absurd risks, you get to have a close inspection of at least one photo.

Even with this change in acceptability, I'm sure most singles have stated loudly and without qualification: 'You wouldn't see me dead browsing one those depressing sites.' I also used to feel they were somewhat desperate and dodgy but so too is hanging around in bars. So, after one too many drinks and too many quiet nights, I found myself trawling through various sites, purely for educational purposes.

By my reading, sites fall into two categories. First are the sites looking to facilitate singles who want to be romantically connected, in other words sites I consider reputable. Second are those sites, such as Ashley Madison, well known for all the wrong reasons, that are interested in facilitating anyone looking for a *physical* connection. It's a subtle difference but usually the site name gives it away. Or the pseudonyms and photos may leave little to the imagination. My research was both educational and an eye opener.

The path I took with online dating was, I think, probably typical. I perused the sites for a short period but it wasn't long before I took the next step and registered. The main reason for this is that you get access to more detailed information about the individuals on the site who may have caught your eye. More than this though, you have to develop your own profile that others can see unless, like me, you choose to keep it hidden. Registering seemed a harmless step and I hardly noticed that the site was drawing me in, spider-like, with my credit card looking like a fly.

Registering makes you a part of the site and gives you access to more details but not to all the information or privileges you need to engage meaningfully with anyone. It's a taste but you're not allowed to touch. At this point I had to choose between retreating or spending some money – and I reckon the conversion rate of registering to paying would be high. Like swimming, once you've put your toe in the water you're going to dive in eventually.

I reached the point where I thought, what's the worst that could possibly happen? Prising out my credit card, I came out of the dark and exposed myself, again figuratively, to what I imagined was a throng of enthusiastic, single woman.

I joined a 'wholesome' site but even then I initially remained firmly in the shadows. I didn't upload a photo and ignored winks and requests from people who wanted to see what I looked like. My rationale was that I'd be recognised and it would get out and that would be embarrassing. It didn't take me long before I realised that when profiles, like mine, don't have a photo, you suspect the worst, a munter. It's the bar-room equivalent of sitting with a paper bag on your head hoping someone takes an interest. I looked only at profiles with photos and I assumed that's what most people did.

Before coming out, so to speak, I first needed to select a decent and representative photo. You don't need a degree in marketing to realise that the photo you select should show you in your best possible light. This is your chance to get people to do that double take. This was blindingly obvious – but it was regularly ignored if you look at the photos often selected.

IMAGE 101

I feel the need to branch out here and offer some legitimate tips. Do not select a photo where you are: staring blankly or frowning (uninspiring), heavily pixelated (suspect), holding alcohol (booze hag or hound), holding your child (feels awkward), smoking (it's not the seventies) or looking like the photo has come from your police file. These are sure-fire ways to get people hurriedly clicking 'next'. In addition, selfies (unless you manage to snap a great one and they're rare), wearing sunglasses (they don't make you look cool), old black-and-white photos (it's still not the seventies) and strange clothes or fancy dress (eccentric and not in a good way) all cast doubts about your appearance and judgement. In this day and age, in which every device has a camera, if you haven't got a recent nice, natural photo of yourself looking happy and at your best, get a friend or your children to snap fifty photos and pick a decent one. Give yourself a fighting chance.

Also, when you write your brief bio, that's the two sentences that people will read first. Make sure you have it proofread. I'm a long way from being a stickler when it comes to spelling and grammar, though thankfully I have a proofreader who isn't, but it's off-putting to think the attractive-looking person in the photo is illiterate. So if you can't spot the problems in the following verbatim examples, please get someone else to check what you've written. I know my proofreader will twitch while reading them, unable to scar them with red pen or track changes.

- *i am a people person, love meeting new people, i love cooking,gardening,wining and dining, going to the movies and shows. have two lovely daughters,a dog ,and two cats.*
- *Fill time mum, Who puts her kids first,They are my life. Im someone who always lends a helping hand to family, friends, and community.*
- *Oh my, this is hard SO il keep it brief and to the point. *Ive just come out of a 20+ yr relationship.*

Once you have chosen a decent photo, proofread your bio, paid your money and clicked 'Show me to the world', interest in you is likely to soar. Now the experience becomes addictive because you can see how many times you have been viewed and by whom. I found myself checking regularly. Interest, in the form of messages, increased and I started engaging in a number of online conversations, some with people in whom I was interested but many that I wasn't.

I quickly learned that the normal rules of etiquette don't apply in the online dating world. Generally if someone walks up to you and says 'Hello' you reciprocate and start chatting. Online it seems the protocol is to simply ignore messages from people you aren't interested in. The reason for this is that in the online world things can advance quickly and before you know it you're being asked out for coffee. More offence is likely to be taken if you say 'Sorry, you're not my type'. It's preferable, apparently, to electronically turn your back without a word.

In among the messages and conversations there were people who sparked my interest. However, I learnt that before you let things progress any further, first do your homework. Most people who have profiles on online dating sites will likely also have a presence on other social media sites such as Facebook, Twitter or LinkedIn. Although you may not have his or her full name, and you're mad, keen or both if you ask someone out before you know their real name, there's usually enough information on their profile or in your conversations to feed into Google. It definitely pays to see what else is out there. At the very minimum you'll likely discover more up-to-date photos! A number of times I was able to work out who I was chatting to and find out enough information that allowed me to work out whether I wanted to continue on or not.

That brings up another vital point: you need to have a fair idea of what, and who, you're looking for. On reflection one of my mistakes was to work on the basis of initial attraction and see what happened from there. It may sound shallow but it seemed the logical thing to do at the time. I looked to engage with those I found attractive based on the photos they'd submitted together with any others I could dig out. Then, if we got on conversationally online, I'd see what happened from there. This replicates a bar-room pick-up and misses the opportunity to be more discerning. If, for example, you like staying in and watching TV then engaging with someone who is a dedicated kick boxer and marathon runner will probably mean there'll be compatibility issues.

Ultimately, like me, you'll take the big step and ask someone out or you'll be asked out.

This isn't a guide to internet security, but never, never give out your contact details until you're absolutely sure you want to have continued contact with this person. A few times I was given a mobile number immediately with a 'Please text me' and they were people I chose to ignore immediately. It didn't feel right swapping that sort of information so early. If you text or email someone then they'll have your mobile number or email address. While it's easy enough today to block them, why make life painful and icky?

As for an initial meeting location, a mutually agreed public meeting place such as a café is, I found, the easiest and safest option. The majority of people are genuine, but some are best avoided and I'd advise caution until you know enough to be sure.

If you're romantically inclined, like me, then you'll have an idealistic concept of first dates – shy smiles, increased heart rate, furtive looks and a mental thumbs-up after you've given them the once-over. Let me assure you that unless you're particularly lucky or have been particularly thorough, it will be nothing remotely like that.

In hindsight I wish I was the sort of person who takes a quick look at the potential dating situation from a distance and walks away if it doesn't look like an attractive proposition. But sadly – and maybe that should be *thankfully* as it is a rather mercenary approach – I'm not, and so I had some ordinary dates and the odd shocker. Most of the advice I've just given was learned the hard way. In fact, the first date was the worst and I'm surprised that it didn't scare me off online dating for good. She looked nothing like her photo, although to be fair she had warned me in a text that she was 'no oil painting', when I met her in a questionable public bar. Some of her friends who were also there were highly conversationally challenged and everyone, except me, was drinking RTDs like water. I remained for as little time as was polite and got the hell out of there.

What online dating teaches you is patience, scepticism and the ability to see what's there and not what you want to see. The grainy photo may be hiding natural beauty but it's usually grainy for a reason. I think that pessimists are better suited to online dating. They will, at the very least, never be disappointed. If, like me, you're an optimist, you court disillusionment and disaster.

THE DATES

I'm not going to give you a blow-by-blow account of any of my dating experiences as that would make hard reading – and writing. I was actively on the dating scene and sites for about six months before I'd had enough. To give you an idea of what it was like I've summarised my experiences into two generic and fictitious dates: one with Lola and one with Charlotte.

Lola and I exchanged fun and interesting messages for about a week before we decided to meet and see if there was a spark. We arranged to meet for coffee and I got to the café early in order to be relaxed and get a quiet table. Spotting Lola turned out to be difficult as she didn't resemble her photo. It was because she was hesitantly looking around the room that she stood out. I attracted her attention and we introduced ourselves by shaking hands. I did the chivalrous thing and bought coffees and, when I returned to the table, we hesitantly started making conversation.

Lola was pleasant, and we got on well, though the conversation felt slightly strained and uncomfortable. I noticed during lulls that I was clenching my buttocks tightly, which was something I didn't even know I did. We talked about work, our families and mostly about our experiences in the online dating world, which was one of the few things we seemed to have in common.

As the date progressed it became clear that there wasn't a spark and so we politely parted with a kiss on the cheek. There were assurances that we would meet up again but one, or both, knew that wasn't going to happen. On reflection the date with Lola felt closer to being an employer in a job interview in which you make up your mind in the first two minutes and spend the rest of the time justifying your decision. In many respects, though, that's what dating is all about: meeting, testing and, if it don't fit, don't force it.

With Charlotte, on the other hand, there was chemistry and it seemed promising and exciting. The first meeting, again over coffee, was livelier and the conversation flowed with little effort and no buttock clenching. Time went unnoticed and the date finished with a hug and, interestingly, no mention of future dates. I sent a text within thirty minutes saying that I'd enjoyed our date and was keen to see more of her if she was interested. Charlotte also replied quickly and we started dating.

The dates were fun whether we ate out, met for a before-work coffee, lunch in the park or took in a local amateur performance of *Macbeth*. Without wishing to kiss and tell, Charlotte and I starting getting on very well. But ... there was something missing or not quite right and after a couple of weeks the dates petered out. There was no animosity – with the odd exception – and we simply headed off in our different directions. One of the most difficult aspects of these dates was finishing them and moving on. Nobody likes to be told, or having to tell someone, that it isn't really what they were hoping for. My preferred method is to just let things lapse, but that's not what adults do. In the end I found honesty was the easiest method, sort of like pulling the plaster off in one quick action.

I kept in contact with some of the Charlottes as friends, but contact became more sporadic over time. You need more than a previous mutual attraction to keep things going. I think, actually I know, that my times with the Charlottes were haunted by the spectre of Cathy, and this factor didn't help. You should never compare your current beau with any of your previous partners, but it's hard not to.

RETREAT

It was after no particular Lola or Charlotte that I happily took down my profile and slid off the dating site and I've never been back. It takes time and energy to be 'in the market', especially online, and I'd run out of steam. The nerves and excitement at the prospect of dating had been replaced by a weary indifference. I felt like a bank teller at the end of an exceedingly long day. Next.

During dating I started to hear comments like 'You seem really relaxed'. I always answered with a polite and surprised (but feigned) 'Really?' I avoided the honest, but unlikely to be well received, answer of 'I'm really not that bothered any more'. This didn't mean that I wasn't interested, or that the date might not end up being promising, but I was a long way from being on the edge. I remained polite and optimistic to the end but I knew it was time to abandon ship.

You hear stories of people finding love online and I'm sure there are many of them, but I didn't sense that carrying on was going to lead to a happy-ever-after. Maybe you do have to be in to win but I was at the point where I couldn't be bothered being in *or* winning. In fact it was a relief to just be single again. I didn't have to worry about scheduling dates, replying to messages or spending time online trawling through mug shots and bios. After a while many of the online faces looked too familiar, as though we were imprisoned together on a really, really bad reality TV show.

I learnt a lot from my dating experiences, including terms like 'friends with benefits' which I'd never encountered before. How the world had changed in the two decades since I was last in a single person's shoes. Significantly, I rediscovered enjoying time on my own. When I separated, my lawyer, who was also recently separated, told me that I would learn to love the silence. Although it took a while, she was right. After my relationship with Cathy ended – and earlier as well now I reflect on it – I didn't like being at home by myself. I spent time at the gym and the office to reduce my waking hours in what sometimes felt like solitary confinement. Now, while I still can't say I love being alone, I certainly feel comfortable and there are less-frequent urges to escape. Usually.

I haven't abandoned dating, by the way, I've just stopped looking online though the effect is much the same. I'm back in my relatively static and comfortable circles where meeting new, single females in roughly the right demographic category are rare. Even then, unless I decide to go out on a limb and ask out a relative stranger, my dance card is likely to remain empty. Besides, 'How often do you come to the gym?' or 'Did I see your photo in the university news?' are tough lines to try.

From the perspective of writing this book in a style that my children can comfortably read, this chapter has been the biggest challenge so far. It's unrecognisable from the first draft, which was more R18 than family friendly. The difficulty is balancing the need to provide enough detail with preventing you, my children and me cringing. In his book *It Takes Balls* Josh Wolf happily goes into intimate detail, so if you're more interested in the confessions of a single dad, pick up a copy of his book. Los Angeles is undoubtedly racier than Palmerston North and I've certainly not had close encounters with seven-foot Puerto Rican prostitutes, but I'm sure it's mainly variations on a theme. People are people, dates are dates.

I'll leave you with what I believe is the biggest lesson I learnt from my time dating. If you suspect the person you're dating isn't the person for you, disentangle yourself as soon as you can *without* being unkind. It's only by staying single that you give yourself a chance of seeing the person you should meet. You'll miss them otherwise — your antennae aren't as big or as powerful as you would like to believe. In the meantime, kick back, relax and enjoy your time by yourself. You may find that it is the best of times.

Reflections

- *Long-distance relationships have a finite life expectancy.*
- *Meeting new attractive and available people is a rare occurrence through normal circumstances and unlikely in bars.*
- *Online dating gives you access to a pool of new people but it needs to be treated with caution. Sites specialise in different areas of the courting spectrum, so tread carefully.*

- Before asking out someone you've met online, or agreeing to go out, see what you can find out about them on other social media sites. Try to see who they are and not who you want them to be.
- Be extremely fussy about who you decide to date. A healthy dose of pessimism is not a bad approach to take and keep to the maxim 'Never sleep with anyone crazier than yourself'.
- Keeping your children unaware of your dates, if you can, is preferable. It allows you to explore the dating scene without the complexity of explaining to your children what you're up to.
- And ... you're better off single than dating someone in whom you have no real interest. Celebrate and enjoy being single!

22. Escaping

Oh, yes, I can cope, dear. Coping's easy. Not puréeing your loved ones, that's the difficult part.
Basil Fawlty (John Cleese, comedian)

The human brain is an interesting and complex organ and it's strange what it decides, on your behalf, to vividly remember amongst all your experiences and adventures. Seemingly trivial experiences and events are stuck in my mind from decades ago yet some mornings I can't remember where I left my car keys. Maybe our brains have more insight about what's important than we realise.

I was twenty and going on a date with Jenny, at least I think that's her name as it was years ago when I worked at the Motor Registration Centre. Those were pre-computer days when everything was captured on paper and dutifully kept in a labyrinth of files. It was an excellent place to work as a twenty-year-old male as there were roughly fifteen females for every male in the building. Useful odds, and I earned my money shuffling paper from one place to another in between 'chatting'.

It was Friday evening and I was picking up Jenny from her home where she lived with her mum – a single mum, I discovered – and two sisters. I was hoping that she'd answer the door so we could do an immediate exit, but it was her mum who greeted me and, dragging me into the lounge, insisted that we stay for a few minutes. I recall the house was extremely ordered with every available flat surface, horizontal and vertical, decorated with family photos. This isn't unusual but it felt a trifle over the top.

Jenny dominated the conversation. Not Jenny herself but Jenny as a topic via her mum who kept on, and on, and on, pointing to the various pictures of her as a tot, child, young girl or teenager and extolling her looks and demeanour. I sat there smiling, undoubtedly with my buttocks firmly clenched, as it was heavy weather. I didn't need to see the bottle of gin on the kitchen bench to realise her mum was the worse for wear. Mercifully, for both Jenny and I, we didn't hang around long but I remember thinking: why would anyone be worse for wear by 7.30!

Fast forward to the present and I now fully understand how and why alcohol can be a factor at home early in the evening. And it certainly isn't restricted to Friday night. The only difference between Jenny's mum and myself is that my children are likely to be with Rose and, if they are with me, I don't yet have to entertain prospective suitors. That'll change in a few short years and I'd like to believe I will create a memorable impression for the right reasons. If Jenny's mum was a full-time single mum, which in the 1980s was likely, she couldn't go out and leave her children, and if she fancied a drink or three, doing so at home was her only option. On reflection it's really sad, but it's understandable.

DRINKING PATTERNS

Alcohol, and its associated problems, plays a big part in New Zealand culture as it does in most Western countries. I was exposed to alcohol at a relatively young age and I've been drinking, mainly in moderation, for most of my adult life. I think it's because alcohol is so readily available that I've never had the desire to try other drugs. Honestly. I know if I ever get randomly stopped by customs and they ask 'When was the last time you took drugs?' my answer of *'Never'* will doubtlessly not be believed and I'll soon hear the frightening snap of rubber gloves.

It was through writing this book that I realised that my alcohol consumption changed quite significantly when I separated. I started doing something that I'd never done before, drinking when I was alone. The reason for this was simple – it was the first time in my life that I'd really been alone. Previously I'd lived with my parents, then with various flatmates, the odd period back home due to a lack of cash, and finally with Rose. In all these settings alcohol was consumed but there were always people to consume it with. Alcohol was part of the social world.

When you're alone, without even the bored eye of a flatmate to take an interest, nobody knows how much you've drunk. I call it inconspicuous consumption and it applies even when your children are at home – up until the point they're old enough to realise what you're doing. If there's no one present able to comprehend your behaviour and make a judgement – that is, you're drinking too much or you're drunk – then your consumption and its effects go unobserved. If this continues for any length of time then it's more likely to become habitual. The concept applies to any vice or dodgy hobby, like train-spotting. It's a slippery slope.

As well as its well-known negative impact on health, alcohol is also a thief of time. If I have a couple of drinks I usually end up on the couch watching TV. Productive pastimes such as work or writing are shelved. It doesn't have to be a lot of alcohol. A relatively modest amount affects me the next day. According to my recollection from my early university studies, this is to do with alcohol impacting on the sleep cycle. The result is that I don't feel as sharp mentally and it's easier to tackle tasks that don't require deep thinking or concentration.

Physically it's easy to disguise an over-indulgent night. I'm the only one who knows that I'm operating at less than 100 per cent.

After a shower, I appear to the world as though I've leapt out of bed ready to embrace the challenges of the new day with a spring in my step. The world doesn't get to see the state of the kitchen or the overflowing glass recycle bin. I've heard of people putting their empties in their neighbour's bins to cover their tracks. The fact that nobody will notice or care is beside the point. Remember, the key word is inconspicuous and an over-flowing glass bin of empties is hardly that.

WHY DRINK?

So why bother to drink at all? That's a question I've asked myself on a number of occasions. The obvious solution is to just stop, but it isn't quite that simple. I think the answer is because it's easier, and more socially acceptable, to drink than to not drink. New Zealand and Western culture looks on those who abstain unkindly. They're the boring people who don't know how to have a good time. The key word that needs to be added to drinking is moderation but that's also harder than it sounds as New Zealand also has a solid culture and reputation for binge drinking.

You don't need to be a psychologist to understand that most vices are coping-and-escape mechanisms. They're short-term tickets off the planet and, thankfully, they're normally return tickets. Your cares dull and sometimes disappear completely, at least for a while. The programmes on TV are hilarious and you feel like you are back on top of your game. The euphoria alcohol provides is similar to other drugs because alcohol is a drug. We don't call it that because we, society, like to delude ourselves that alcohol is respectable. Drugs, on the other hand, are evil and people who take them are, well, druggies.

It's simply a social construct, a perception that society through laws and behaviours agrees to observe. Alcohol, drinking and even being drunk in some circumstances (e.g. weddings) is acceptable. Taking drugs, being stoned or wasted is not. History, through periods such as prohibition, tells us that the current state of affairs is not permanent and that change will occur. History also tells us that changing the law often has little impact on what people do. Prohibition didn't stop people drinking, it just reclassified them as criminals. It also allowed gangsters to establish themselves and make a lot of money, that's an example of the law of unintended consequences in operation.

Policy makers appear ignorant of the law of unintended consequences and are shocked when what happens isn't what they expect. In New Zealand, a law shutting pubs at 6pm was promoted as a way of ensuring that men got home to their families at a respectable hour. They did, but they were often smashed from drinking as much as possible in the hour between work finishing and the pubs closing. What was intended to reduce alcohol consumption instead gave us the charming social effects of the six-o'clock swill and the drunk-train and helped establish our binge-drinking culture.

CUTTING BACK

Once I recognised that I was drinking too much, and that the pattern of drinking alone wasn't healthy, I decided that I needed to make some changes. Initially I did try to simply 'go on the wagon', but I soon realised that option didn't fit my lifestyle. I didn't want to give up drinking, I just wanted to return to social drinking. This was harder than I thought because the reasons why my drinking habits had changed hadn't gone away. I was still single, and evenings without the children remained quiet and solitary. To make the required lifestyle changes required more effort than willpower alone. There are bound to be stronger-willed people than I who stop after one or two even if the sun is scorching, the fridge is full of ice-cold beer and nobody's watching. Unfortunately that doesn't appear to be me.

Before I go on I need to point out that I am not talking about, or suffering from, alcoholism. I'm fairly confident of that, though I'm also fairly confident that I used to drink more than is healthy.

There's a big difference. The adjustments I made worked for me, in the main, but in keeping with this book, they are not meant to be a recipe to follow. The logic is, try a lot of things, see what works, keep doing those things and forget the rest.

The first thing I did was reduce the amount of alcohol in the house. With lots of beer in the fridge it's too easy to have one too many. It may also be a male trait that the amount we drink is in direct proportion to the amount available. I was chatting about this at karate with my sparing partners and we appeared to be similar. If we buy a dozen beer we're likely to drink more than if we buy a six-pack. Enforced restraint by limiting what alcohol is in the house I found to be a useful tactic.

I also avoided stocking up on duty-free spirits if I happened to be returning from overseas. That's an easy trap to fall into just because they're cheap. I don't need a fully stocked bar to cater for the trickle of visitors I have and I don't need to stock the range of spirits required to make drinks that require umbrellas and swizzle sticks.

Making sure I drink in moderation when the children are with me I found to be a great policy. When they're smaller and don't understand the effect of alcohol you can probably get away with it, but as they grow they soon realise what's going on. I can't claim to be a saint in this regard but I avoid going too far. It's in no one's best interests for children to see their parents sozzled and mine have never had to witness me in that state. It's a critical line in the sand as I'm the most significant male role model in their lives. When Cathy had her children with her, she always remained sober enough to drive them to the hospital in an emergency. It's a great benchmark to aim for.

Another tactic I employed was to increase the number of gym sessions I attended. This works for two reasons. First, after I exercise I feel less like drinking, which is a mental thing rather than a reduction in desire. My reasoning is that it doesn't make any sense to expend all that energy on exercise to negate it through drinking and having an alcohol-inspired kebab and baklava. Second, that reasoning doesn't always work and at least the exercise negates the drinking, kebab and baklava. It's a dollar each way.

Eating is a good tactic to employ. Once I eat dinner I don't feel like drinking and with no over-flowing drinks cabinet to provide a *digestif* I don't drink and I find other things to do. With the children this is easy as they are always starving and this encourages eating early. Without them I focus on ensuring that dinner is organised in advance or I bring takeaways home.

Lastly, I found other things to do with my time in the evening that would normally be at the mercy of drinking, namely writing, study and work. The addition of alcohol is almost guaranteed to root me to the couch to watch sport or reruns of *QI* (easily the best show on TV). I found that when I have writing to look forward to I abstain to ensure I'm mentally fit for the challenge. It also meant I *was* able to leap out of bed, ready to embrace the challenges of the new day with a spring in my step. In other words, I created a virtuous cycle rather than a vicious one.

Finally, and maybe most importantly, when all these tactics failed, when I wanted to take the easy way out and escape, the biggest thing I did was to *not* beat myself up. I would wake the next morning and give myself a mental cuddle rather than a good kicking. I clean the kitchen, brew some strong coffee and start again.

If you're anything like me you'll have a queue of people in your life ready to find fault, criticise and generally make you feel guilty and unworthy. The last thing you should ever do is join that queue. I like the way Arianna Huffington, of the *Huffington Post* fame, described it when she said it was like having an obnoxious roommate in your head. So try talking to yourself as though you were talking to your best friend. 'It's okay, you're fine.' Or 'It happens when you are under a lot of pressure, it's no big deal, you can still have a great day'. Not the roomie from hell, 'What the feck were you thinking, you eejit?'. Or 'You ought to be ashamed, you are without doubt a gobshite parent'. I have no idea why but my obnoxious roommate seems to be Irish.

Writing the majority of this book has been fun, but this chapter, together with a couple of others that didn't make the cut, has been a test. In that regard my writing has roughly followed my experience of single parenting – in the main it's been fun, an adventure, albeit unplanned. But there are a couple of areas that I would have preferred to sweep under the carpet, out of sight, out of mind. However, an account that included only the positive aspects and ignored the harder subjects and times would be false. A memoir through rose-tinted spectacles.

I think most single parents will probably recognise aspects of this chapter in their own lives, whether they like to have the occasional drink or more. When the going gets tough, most of the time I'm able to rise to the challenge and emerge, win, lose or draw, better for the experience. But occasionally I wave the white flag and live to fight another day.

Reflections

- *Escape, via alcohol (or other means), can be tempting when pressure builds but try and make the trips few and far between.*
- *When you become a single parent, with no one around to judge, your drinking habits can deteriorate.*
- *If you recognise you are drinking too much and can simply stop or return to your previous level, great. If not, make some changes in your life to help such as:*
  - *Reduce the amount of alcohol available.*
  - *Find activities to do to occupy the quiet times*
  - *Exercise more. This will at least help counter any excesses.*
- *If you over-indulge from time to time, don't beat yourself up. Treat yourself as your own best friend.*

23. In the Thick of Things

The things that matter most must never be at the mercy of the things that matter least.
Johann Goethe (writer and philosopher, 1749-1832)

Rog, now fourteen, had an upcoming piano exam during a week he was at Rose's. The piano and the ability to practise was, however, at my house. This didn't present a problem as Rog is very responsible and we arranged that on Wednesday and Thursday he would walk to my house after school, let himself in and practise until Rose turned up after work.

I came home on Wednesday around 6.30pm after the gym and I found the house as expected. It was exactly as I'd left it apart from an empty ginger beer bottle and various discarded snack food wrappers on the bench. No surprise there. The one change I hadn't anticipated was that Rog had turned on his computer. I assumed that after he had practised for what he considered to be a sufficient length of time, he'd taken a break and played a game or surfed the net. Maybe Rose had been late. It has been known to happen.

To encourage him to focus on the task at hand, and to make sure he knew that I didn't miss anything, I left a note on his computer: 'This is not a piano!!!' I signed the note with a winking smiley face so he knew I wasn't serious or annoyed.

The next day the house was once again as expected. Another empty ginger beer bottle and accompaniments in the kitchen and the computer had once again been turned on. This time there was a note on my desk: 'It's a metaphorical piano.' Rog signed it with the same winking smiley face.

Now I'm not entirely sure that his use of the word metaphorical was appropriate, but I wasn't about to challenge that aspect because my English and grammar is what I'd describe as tradesman-like. The point I'm trying to make is that your children go from being innocent and unknowing to incredibly clever and wise beyond their years seemingly overnight. When they were little I didn't have to try hard to keep one step ahead of them. They believed everything Rose and I told them, evidenced by the existence of Santa Claus, the Tooth Fairy and a range of invented characters designed to illicit the desired behaviour, usually sleep.

This is the age when children are arguably at their loveliest. When you play hide and seek, unless you stand in the middle of the room with a lamp on your head, they never find you. And when they hide, their leg is always sticking out ninety degrees from the curtain or the bed, the two places they always choose. This provides you with the opportunity to develop your acting skills – 'Oh forsooth, they've vanished like an old oak table. I fear I will have to summon the local constabulary.' Admittedly it's bad acting but the audience is forgiving. For an extra thrill we sometimes played hide and seek outside at night with torches. This allowed me the opportunity to occasionally explode from my hiding place just to hear Liv's soprano scream. I'm amazed the neighbours never called the police.

If you can't stay one step ahead of your children when they're little, you're just not trying. Cathy once famously put the clocks forward an hour because she was feeling sick, which hurried her two off to bed early. If the Tooth Fairy catches me out, which he or she often did, and the children emerged in the morning looking disappointed and cashless, I would invent some vaguely plausible ruse to distract them while putting money under their pillow. 'You see, you just didn't look hard enough!' After they wised up to the non-existence of the Tooth Fairy, I told them that she still might deliver at Mum's house so don't rip your tooth out, as Liv liked to do, until you're there.

STAYING RELEVANT

But there comes a point in time, quicker than you'd hope, when there's little to be gained in trying to put one over on your children. From the day Rog, and therefore Liv, understood how the world worked, trying to pull the wool over their eyes became an exercise in futility. And it gets worse. With their new-found knowledge and confidence they're not only aware, they also discover they too have the power of stealth and deception.

After I'd put the children to bed, it must have been around Christmas, I was still hungry so I nipped into the kitchen. I spied the Christmas mince pies and quietly, as cellophane wrappers tend to make a racket, I eased one out. I hadn't realised that Liv had followed me and was now hiding, and watching, from the alcove next to the kitchen. I must have been hungry because I shoved the whole thing in my mouth – they were only small – and nearly choked when she leapt out. 'Caught you,' she hissed, imitating Gollum (we'd been working our way through the *Lord of the Rings* films). Then, as a result of my overstuffed mouth, she added Gollum-style, 'Ohhhh the fat one, he eats it whole.'

If you tell little white lies past this point in your children's development you can get yourself into trouble on the credibility front. I learnt this from an example that thankfully wasn't mine, it was Rose's. She told the children that as she'd started her new job in Wellington she couldn't take time off to look after them in the holidays. Plausible and accepted – until two months later, having forgotten her earlier groundwork, she told them she was taking off for a week when she didn't have them because she needed a break. Wheels and cogs turn quickly in my children's heads. I don't know what the repercussions were but I know that in the next school holidays she took the week off. My children, Rog especially, have memories like elephants and have no problem playing the guilt card mercilessly. Here's a saying worth remembering: always tell the truth, it's easier to remember.

When the children reached this more knowing age my philosophy recognised that it was time to stop treating them as the children. Not that I think you should treat them as a fully formed adults, not yet, but more in the manner of adults with training wheels. To do this I didn't develop a plan to guide how we interacted, I didn't even have a vague idea. I could've read one of the myriad of books on parenting tweenies and teenagers written by 'experts' who have researched the field and come up with sound, sensible advice. That would have given me some ideas to try, but with the benefit of hindsight I don't think they're necessary.

As my children became more confident our relationship evolved naturally to match the altered situation. On reflection, it became evident that this happened simply because I was closely involved in my children's lives. I was in step and that meant that when things needed to be tweaked, they were tweaked. If you aren't in step then your relationship will probably feel more like a series of staggered, and staggering, lurches as you periodically try to catch up. In between times the communication gap between you and your children will grow and you'll lose relevance and gain frustration. This is a phenomenon often brushed off as 'You can't talk to teenagers'. You can't if you don't know what's important in their lives. They're maturing and you're being left behind.

I was talking with a married male friend who related an incident that he'd had with his thirteen-year-old son. The story itself isn't important, it was his perception of the situation and how he handled it that I found intriguing. To cut to the chase, he told me that he realised he was still treating his son as a small child. When this dawned on him he decided to treat him like an adult. It was good that he recognised the problem but I think his action was too much of a leap. From listening closely, I got the impression the relationship went from parent-child to something closer to manager-employee overnight. That has to be confusing. In theory a manager-employee relationship is an adult-adult relationship, but it's often not because most managers think and act like teachers.

Apart from the speed of change, another important point from this story is that treating your children more like adults shouldn't equal treating them more like just *any* adult. That's like treating your partner like any other woman or man and the reason that's unlikely to go down well is because it's dumb. You need to treat your children like the very special soon-to-be adults that they are to you.

I didn't do anything in particular to change the way I treated Rog and Liv and we navigated and negotiated our way through these years together. I couldn't treat them identically either. Apart from them being a boy and a girl, Rog was older and therefore needed more latitude. As younger siblings do, Liv grew quicker by learning from Rog's example but our relationship was still different. Like the previous observation, trying to have the same relationship with all your children is also dumb because they're individuals. There are many aspects that will be common, but many others will be substantially different. It's not one size fits all, even if you have twins!

I appreciate that this may be hard advice to heed because it isn't a simple recipe of doing A, B, C and D and Bob's your uncle. Self-help books are appealing because they're sold on this basis: they tell you their generic solution and all you have to do is implement it successfully, which is usually impossible. They have that TV shopping channel formulaic feel to them: 'For only $99 plus postage and handling get the ten-minute parent workout, a sure-fire short cut to a wonderful and fulfilling relationship with your children'.

There aren't short cuts and it's only hard work if you make it hard work. If you're fully engaged with your children you'll all enjoy the good old days you'll remember and they don't last for long. Soon enough they'll turn into fully formed adults and will be heading out into the world.

There are fathers – I'm using that term deliberately than the warmer term 'dads', who will end up wondering why their adult children don't have a lot of time for them. They'll hear from them on their birthday, Christmas, maybe Father's Day if their spouse reminds them, or if they need money, but seldom else. No dropping in or unexpected phone calls because they just want to talk. Harry Chapin's song 'Cats in the Cradle' describes this situation succinctly. There's a massive difference between staying in touch because you feel you should – an obligation – and because you want to, which is friendship. Fathers who believe that they can make up for lost time by having more to do with their children when they're older are, I think, in the main going to be disappointed.

In saying that, it's never too late to get closer to your children if you're doing it for the right reasons. You can't change the past and you can only influence the future. The day you become aware of why the gap between you exists is the day you can start doing something about it. I wouldn't suggest bounding back into your children's lives like a reborn Ebenezer Scrooge. I'd start by taking a greater interest and communicating on a regular basis for no reason. It takes time to develop a relationship; biological considerations gain you few, if any, Brownie points.

I suspect that the underlying problem for many fathers, and far fewer mothers, is that they haven't come to terms with the concept that when you have children you no longer come first, your children do. Always. I empathise with parents who, through personal circumstances, aren't able to be around as much as they'd like, but those who choose to be absent, who prioritise work and their own interests, or take time for themselves when they could be spending it with their children, will one day have a lot of time to reflect. Maybe that's what they wanted.

TRUST

Having a close relationship with your children as they develop means your life as a parent becomes easier, not harder. This is because the relationship is built on trust. I trust my children to act responsibly, but maintain a wary eye for signs that I need to intervene. They trust me to be fair and consistent. As previously noted, trust is fundamental in all adult relationships and without it you're back in the playground. In my first 'real' job we were managed like children and so, when the manager left the building, we acted like children and started playing cricket in the corridor and generally goofing around. When we saw his or her car return, we scrambled back to our desks and looked busy.

Please, however, don't think I have it completely sorted and my children act perfectly and like adults all the time. They don't. They're adults-in-training and I still have to be a parent from time to time. I police bedtime and the biscuit jar, nag about clothes and drag them away from the computers and screens. But if I need to, I can trust them to put themselves to bed or turn their light off after half an hour's reading. They manage their own homework, know the chores they need to do and I can leave them at home, now they are old enough, without fear that I'll come home to a nightmare.

When I came back from overseas, just before I succumbed to jet-lag I explained that I would get dessert after I rested my eyes for five minutes. I woke up fresh as a daisy at 3am to find that they'd eaten dessert, put the plates in the kitchen and were tucked up in bed asleep. They would have brushed their teeth as well. My children have worked out that there are times that they must act responsibly and times when the world is fair game.

Money is an area that I think can indicate how much trust you've developed with your children. I keep containers on my desk for loose change as it weighs down my pockets. I don't count it and I've no idea how much is there. Rog and Liv dip into this when they need it for school although they always ask. I told them, when I showed them the containers, that I trusted them 100 per cent. If it didn't work out, I would change the system. My hunch is that they prefer to be thought of as trustworthy and treated like an adult.

Slightly more daringly, they also know the pin number of my bank card and credit card. Once they knew one they knew them all as like 99 per cent of the population, I have one number for all my cards. I didn't plan to give it to them, it happened because during its all-too-frequent use they picked up the number. I don't see it as an issue and I can't be bothered having to remember a different number, although it did create an interesting situation in the supermarket.

'Can I pay?' Liv asked.

'Sure, where's your wallet?'

'I meant with your card, eejit.' Liv uses the word from *Mrs Brown's Boys* with affection. I think.

'Okay,' and I gave her my bank card which she swiped through the EFTPOS terminal. Just as she went to put in the pin number, a red-faced checkout lady came bustling over.

'She can't pay,' she said loudly and stridently. Liv took a step back and it felt as though we were under a dazzling spotlight. Supermarkets are generally boring places but we were starring in our own 'play for today' and entertaining our fellow shoppers.

'Why would that be?' I asked slowly.

'Because she's buying alcohol and she's underage.'

'No she isn't ...' The checkout lady, minus her checkout, looked confused as my twelve-year-old Liv definitely looked under-aged. I helpfully added, '... buying alcohol that is. I am. It's for me.'

'But she's paying.'

'No, I'm paying, it's my card.'

'Does she know your pin number?'

'Yep.'

'That's madness!'

I smiled and shrugged. There was little point in trying to describe why Liv knowing my pin wasn't a problem. The non-checkout lady was now very confused. She thought for a few seconds before taking us right back to square one as though the previous conversation hadn't happened.

'People under eighteen are not allowed to buy alcohol.'

Some days I would enjoy coolly stepping back through the logic to once again demonstrate that Liv wasn't buying alcohol, but it didn't seem fair. What we were doing just didn't fit in with her normal world order and, after all, the rules are the rules. You can't chip away at the foundations of society – where would it end? Babies would soon be buying cigarettes. You have to pick your battles and this one, while very winnable and maybe fun, wasn't worth fighting.

'Okay. Sorry Liv, I'll need my card.'

Liv, who was somewhat embarrassed by the exchange, handed back my card and I completed the transaction. Liv was thankfully no longer viewed as a criminal and the supermarket's citizens returned to their own important business.

'I'm sorry, but the store has its policies.' She clearly felt obliged to justify her actions.

'Absolutely, it's really no problem,' I assured her and we wandered off.

It'll be interesting to see how my relationship with the children develops as they charge towards full adulthood. A number of people have said to me, no actually they've *told* me: 'It'll change, you won't be able to talk to them and they'll ignore you.' Really? That sounds defeatist and generally depressing advice. I doubt it's a hard-and-fast rule of life that a generation gap is mandatory, even in the technology-fuelled age in which we live.

It's easy enough to allow a gap to develop and it's hard to bridge when you're busy, but I often come back to Goethe's quote that started this chapter: 'The things that matter most must never be at the mercy of the things that matter least.' It would be easy to get overly fixated on my own life – work, study, this book, rugby league, cricket, Formula One, romance, fitness, movies, reading, drinking, sleeping on the couch, etc. I may think I'm important and in the thick of things, but Goethe reminds me that I'm more likely to be in the thick of *thin* things.

Reflections

- *If you're interested and tuned in to your children you'll remain relevant in their lives.*
- *You need to understand and embrace the concept that your children come first, not you.*
- *Your relationship with your children needs to evolve at the same speed as your children. Don't make the mistake of treating them as children when they are far closer to being adults.*
- *It's never too late to take a full and real interest in your children, though it's best if this starts from when they are born.*
- *Ask yourself whether you would be okay with your children knowing the pin number for your credit card. If the answer is no, why?*
- *Don't let your children buy alcohol for you, society simply isn't ready.*

24. Sons and Daughters

Sugar and spice and all things nice.
That's what little girls are made of.
Snips and snails and puppy-dogs' tails.
That's what little boys are made of.
Nineteenth-century nursery rhyme

If you weren't aware, snips are the odds and ends typically collected by small boys. Nails, screws, heel plates, pens, pencils, rubbers, wrappers and, in Rog's words, interestingly shaped rocks. These snips weighed down his pockets for weeks. Liv doesn't collect snips, or snails for that matter, and I only find forgotten money in Liv's pockets, which I consider a bonus for doing the washing.

It's these differences that are the focus of this chapter. The similarities and dissimilarities I've noticed between raising boys and girls. The differences aren't obvious when the children are small but as they move from tot to tweenie and especially through puberty and into their teens, that's when they started to become more obvious. At least that's what I thought.

I've been mulling over this question ever since I heard Tyler Durden philosophise in *Fight Club* that 'we're a generation of men raised by women'. I've come to the conclusion that my generation was, but I don't think my son's generation will be. That may be wishful thinking. But at the very least my son isn't. He's been raised by both sexes and all that took was for me to be as interested and engaged as Rose and that was easy. I'm sure there's research that will back up my commonsense opinion that boys grow into more rounded, confident men with good, solid, calm male role models in their life. As a dad you're a vital piece of the puzzle, irrespective of your marital status, as long as you remain a positive role model. Children don't need erratic, fragile and frantic role models.

Although we're all products of our own history and environment, equally I think we have the ability to change and evolve. George Santayana, a twentieth-century philosopher, said those who don't remember the past are doomed to repeat it. He wasn't referring just to individuals but to societies, countries and the world. Dads from previous generations have powerful lessons for us, good and bad. My own dad was part wonderful and part absent, and I hope I have embraced the wonderful and learned how not to be absent. It was the thinking of the time that dads got involved in parenting when a good telling-off was required. I say this quite neutrally and I don't harbour any resentment against my dear old dad, who passed away gently about a decade ago. It was simply the way it was. But I think I've learnt that this method was inherently flawed and you end up becoming something akin to the family bouncer.

BOYS WILL BE BOYS

Returning to the current generation, I'd like to say that it's more an old-fashioned stereotype that sees boys as relatively slovenly with a poor eye for detail. Actually I'd like not to, but Rog confirms this stereotype on a daily if not hourly basis. His clothes are always stored in a piled, jumbled mess. The pockets of his school trousers remain full of rubbish, although when I suggested that this was the case, he denied it saying actually only the front-left pocket was for rubbish. 'The other pockets are for items of value.'

The clincher for me came at the start of the school year when

Rog was fourteen. I bought him a new school bag as the last two had each lasted barely six months. I gave him his new bag with the instructions 'I'm tossing your old bags out as they've had it. Can you go through them and make sure there's nothing in them?'

'Yep,' Rog said without taking his eyes from the hoard of zombies his character was busily cutting a swathe through. About thirty minutes later Rog emerged from his room and dropped the bags in front of me.

'Checked, emptied and ready for the trash?' I politely inquired.

'Yep.' My teenage boy is not verbose, which I'm sure is common.

I picked up the bags and I was about to head outside to complete the task when I stopped and turned to look closely at Rog.

'You've gone through these thoroughly?' I asked suspiciously.

'Yep.'

'You do know what the word *thorough* means, don't you?'

'Yes,' Rog answered with an exaggerated smile.

'You don't mind if I check them?'

'Be my guest.' At last something resembling a sentence.

I went through the bags and when I'd finished I sat back and exclaimed, 'And what do we have here, Ali Baba?' Rog appeared, all in one teenage look, unimpressed, confused and sheepish. From the two bags, checked and certified devoid of anything useful, I found: $7.50, a pair of clean socks, a ruler, a pop-up umbrella and an unpresented cheque for his school for $22. Unbelievable!

Rog's lack of attention to detail is worsening as he embraces his teenage status. Very recently we took a short holiday and I instructed Rog and Liv what they needed to take in the way of clothes. I must shoulder some of the blame for not checking his heavy bag, but I was staggered when I found that rather than packing for the trip, he just didn't unpack his clothes from when he was dropped off. So his bag contained five times the clothes needed, including his full set of cricket gear. The saying 'Boys will be boys' doesn't do Rog justice sometimes.

Liv, on the other hand, does her bit for female stereotypes by adoring and collecting teddy bears, as I've described. She has hundreds and seems to be able to remember all their names. She still sleeps with a chosen few. Brown teddy was her first-ever teddy bear, Lee was from Leeds castle, there's Soffy, whose name is a mystery to me, Cute is a tiger from Dream World, Eeyore was a birthday present from Euro-Disney and Doughnut she got as a present when she was ill. Collecting and looking after teddy bears was Liv's keenest hobby until she hit puberty.

PUBERTY

Puberty, that's a difficult subject at the best of times. It marks the point when boys and girls charge off in differing, erratic directions and your parenting needs to diversify and evolve to keep up. Before puberty I think you can raise boys and girls pretty much the same and treat them based on their own varied personalities. Sports, rough-and-tumble times, chores, movies, responsibilities, money and bedtime are all much of a muchness. There are variations required due to age but not many, I think, due to gender. Puberty tips that situation on its head.

As a parent I wasn't looking forward to my children going through puberty let alone them coming out the other side. Right up to that stage children are, well, children. Mostly cute, funny, short, easy going, early to bed, chatty – and they think you know everything. Puberty marks the time when they transition into awkward, tall, difficult, demanding, late-to-bed mini-adults – who think *they* know everything.

I was more daunted by the impact of puberty on Liv as, like I am sure the vast majority of men, my experience in matters of 'women's health' is extremely limited. It's not a topic of conversation that men are included in and, as a general rule, I think we're satisfied with that. So at best I can only claim to have a limited, theoretical knowledge of the topic. Liv is not a theoretical concept and therefore it was with some trepidation that the time drew near when I would be confronted with reality.

For those readers who are keen to hear my insight into how single dads cope with the physical aspects of their daughters going through puberty, my sincere apologies. Rose, far better equipped to deal with the subject, handled everything and the subject has literally never been discussed. This obviously suited Liv as otherwise I'm confident she would have included me where necessary.

In respects to boys going through puberty, physically that's mercifully straightforward, though it does force dads to block out their own experiences of what life was like at the equivalent time. The effects of puberty on Rog are now obvious for all to see. He is now almost as tall as me and has hairier legs, something he can thank or blame his mother's genes for. He hasn't quite started shaving regularly yet, the one curse for all well-groomed men, but that looks months away, not years.

CO-PARENTING

Puberty is a clear example of the benefits of co-parenting after separation versus solo parenting. No matter how hard you try, you simply can't be both sexes. I pondered at the time what I would've done without the aid of Rose. I would've needed help and I think I'd have made sure that Liv had females in her life that she could confide in and trust. I've been blessed with brilliant, capable nannies and arranging them to discuss the subject with Liv may have worked well. I would've also bought books for Liv in advance, which I did anyway, and maybe, just maybe, Liv and I may have had a couple of frank, awkward conversations. In the end I think that what actually happened was the preferred solution for everyone. Especially me, if I'm honest!

Co-parenting, if done effectively, removes many of the potential issues that face solo parents. In many respects co-parenting is a continuation of a nuclear family but performed as a parental tag team.

My children have been equally exposed to male and female parental influences, and I would argue strongly that they've had far more dad time than the majority of nuclear families in which abdication and delegation are often the norm.

This area raises an interesting question regarding same-sex parents and whether they have similar issues to solo parents. I can offer only my thoughts as I don't know a same-sex couple who have children where the other parent isn't somewhere in the mix. My suspicion is, as there are likely to be many people that don't believe same-sex couples can raise children effectively, that they do a far better job than the majority of parents and make sure their children are exposed to all required role models. That's just my hunch though.

With Rog and Liv now in the 'almost-adult' category my parenting has had to be tailored for each of them. But when I wrote down a list of the differences and similarities that I'd observed, there were far more similarities than differences. They both need more personal space now – barging into their rooms unannounced, for example, is now a no-no. Indeed their doors, which used to be permanently open, are now often closed and I respectfully knock, sometimes I have to kick, and await an invitation. The exception is in the morning when they're at their most useless and I need to barge in singing.

While both children are now self-sufficient on the surface, neither can prioritise to save themselves despite my constant use of Stephen Covey's popular habit: put first things first. Time management is a skill clearly developed later in life and I'm sure I was equally useless at their age. They leave important things to the last minute, which leaves muggins to rush around and stick his finger in various dykes to save the day.

Similarly, nor can they tidy up after themselves, get to bed on time, take dishes out to the kitchen and still, despite years and years of nagging, change the toilet roll. They share an appetite for screens and social media and so are policed equally. That's a real battle that my generation of parents is fighting – trying to wrest young adults out of the cyber world and into the real world.

More alarmingly, they've both developed titanic appetites. They can demolish snacks at will and still put away their dinner, the anticipated leftovers *and* dessert. Liv in particular cuts herself slices of bread that leave me wondering which is the slice and which is the loaf. Thankfully, neither appear to be putting on weight, and so I'm assuming that this is part of what is universally referred to as a growth spurt. I'm hoping it stops some time soon.

The differences I've noticed are mainly in the interpersonal areas. Rog doesn't hug as much now and our physical interactions are more likely to involve sparring, gutsing – which is a variation of sparring we've developed where you try and jab your opponent in the guts – and wrestling. Disturbingly, I've found of late that my ability to dominate him physically is becoming increasingly problematic. Where I used to subdue him with minimal fuss, now if he doesn't want to be subdued it takes most of my strength to come out on top. I fear that the time when our physical strengths are equal is just around the corner and I won't even contemplate a world where Rog can wrestle *me* to the floor. The other noticeable aspect with Rog is that he's become more reclusive and so I've had to make an extra effort to engage with him.

Liv still enjoys hugs, although this may be because she's also a little younger. Significantly, Liv has found her voice and realised that she can make her presence felt. Shouting and slamming doors, mainly at Rose's house I'm pleased to report, are two of her preferred methods for getting her thoughts across. I have started telling her that 'We aren't shouty people' and 'Your point doesn't become stronger because you yell it'. At the moment it's done in good spirits, and we both still find the humour in it, but something tells me that isn't always going to be the case. No matter what I may encounter I intend to stick to my philosophy of being the calmest person in the room.

The other new areas in Liv's world are make-up and boys. In a short period of time she has amassed an immense supply of make-up items – primarily from Rose obviously as I wouldn't have a clue what to buy – and she delights in activities such as painting her nails. I encourage this activity in a very dad-like way by playfully sneering 'What a girl'. Simultaneously, she's discovered boys, which is every father's worst nightmare. It's still early days and so I don't have a huge amount of experience to fall back on or relate, but I plan to be an adult and not a dumb stereotypical father whose only response is to try to hold back time. Rose and I allow, and help Liv organise, daytime meetings with boys, ensuring there are adults present at all times. I simply cannot refer to them as dates yet.

The differences between raising boys and girls reminds me of one of my favourite sayings and not a management one this time: 'The more it changes, the more it's the same thing'. Yes, there are differences between raising boys and girls, but the basics of parenting don't change and if you're an engaged parent then you will likely take it all in your stride. The main danger is being left behind or, worse, not being in the race at all.

Reflections

- Break from history and make this a generation of children raised by men and women.
- Boys are stereotypically portrayed as messy and not particularly thorough because it seems they are.
- Puberty is a difficult time. If you are a single dad with a daughter(s), depending on your circumstances this is a time that may need careful planning.
- Co-parenting, if organised well, can be arguably more effective than nuclear families for involving both parents in raising children.
- Raising boys and girls is more similar than you may think, even post-puberty.

Epilogue

To leave the world a bit better, whether by a healthy child, a garden patch, or a redeemed social condition; to know even one life has breathed easier because you have lived. This is to have succeeded.
Ralph Waldo Emerson (writer, 1803-82)

INTERIOR (INT). SINGLE HOTEL ROOM – NIGHT
The room is crowded with four beds, three singles and a double. The room lights are out and the only light comes from the TV on which a movie is playing. DAD lies on the double bed between LIV and ROG and they're watching the movie. ROSE lies on a single bed facing away, talking quietly on a mobile phone. The movie finishes.

>**DAD**
>(Loudly)
>Bedtime and teeth.

No one moves. LIV snuggles into DAD.

>**ROSE**
>(Whispering into the phone)
>I have to go, the movie's finished. I love you too.

DAD, hugging himself, mouths I love you too.

>**LIV**
>(Hissed)
>Daaad.

> **ROG**
> (Whispered)
> I'll guts you.

DAD, starts kissing the back of his hand. ROG and LIV pile on top of DAD as he tries to hide under the covers.

> **ROSE**
> (Sitting up)
> Get him.

The battle rages for a minute or two until DAD restores order.

> **DAD**
> (Loudly)
> Okay that's enough. You can have a lot of fun without being silly. Bedtime and teeth.

> **ROG**
> We can't.

> **DAD**
> Why?

> **ROG**
> Because if we go to bed then we can't clean our teeth. You mean teeth and *then* bedtime.

> **LIV**
> Yeah. Eejit.

> **DAD**
> (Holding up fingers to make a 'W')
> Whatever. I suggest you get a wriggle on or else ...

ROG and LIV, already in their pyjamas leap over the beds and exit into the bathroom. They turn the bathroom light on, illuminating the room more.

> **DAD**
> Are you having that bed?

> **ROSE**
> Yep. I don't plan on moving.

> **DAD**
> Cool. I'll have that one.

INT HOTEL BATHROOM – NIGHT

ROG and LIV are nudging each other as they both try and look at themselves in the mirror. ROG stands on tiptoes, allowing him to have an uninterrupted view.

INT SINGLE HOTEL ROOM – NIGHT

ROG emerges first followed quickly by LIV, who turns the light out. They stand together in front of the double bed.

> **ROG**
> So?
>
> **DAD**
> So what?
>
> **ROG**
> So who gets the double bed?
>
> **DAD**
> Me.
>
> **LIV**
> (Somewhat outraged)
> That's not fair, you promised it to me.
>
> **DAD**
> I was only joking, look at your face. LIV has it tonight and ROG, you get it tomorrow night.
>
> **ROG**
> But ...
>
> **DAD**
> (Cutting him off)
> No buts. You know that's fair.

LIV and ROG, who is still frowning, jump into their respective beds. Rose has her eyes closed. DAD hops into his bed and switches off the TV. The room is dark.

> **LIV**
> Goodnight, Dad. Goodnight, Mum.
>
> **DAD & ROSE**
> Goodnight, Liv.
>
> **ROG**
> Goodnight.

DAD & ROSE
Goodnight, Rog.

LIV
Goodnight, Gutty Butty.

ROG
Goodnight, Hobbit.

DAD
Goodnight, John boy.

ROG & LIV
(Rose laughing in the background)
Who?

SCENE FADES – END

That scene shows how far Rose, Rog, Liv and I have come. I don't think we can be called an estranged family, we're a family that lives in altered circumstances. The four of us are able to share a hotel room without any issues or stress for anyone, especially the children. We weren't on holiday, it was a trip we needed to make for a medical reason and having everyone together not only made sense, it was the right thing to do.

My journey as a parent hasn't finished and it'll never be completely over. Whatever their age, I will always see my children as children and feel responsible for their health and happiness. As a parent, you can feel contented only when your children are, for want of a better word, okay. If you put your children's interests ahead of your own, you're standing on solid ground. That may mean what you want personally has to be delayed or even abandoned and that's simply the price you pay for being a parent.

I often daydream of escaping to greener pastures and new adventures, but when the disappointed and disbelieving faces of my abandoned children join those thoughts I'm brought back to reality. The real trick is to set up your life so you can all escape together.

www.ingramcontent.com/pod-product-compliance
Lightning Source LLC
Chambersburg PA
CBHW021401290426
44108CB00010B/336